The
ILLEGAL
From
HOLLAND

Michael Durack

ISBN
978-1-962868-31-0 (Paperback)
978-1-962868-32-7 (eBook)
978-1-962868-30-3 (Hardcover)

The
ILLEGAL
From
HOLLAND

TABLE OF CONTENTS

Foreword

This is a true story. All of the names have been changed, except for mine, Yolande's, my family's and a few very close friends who gave their permission to let me use their names. All the other names in this book are substitutes to make sure no one is embarrassed for any reason.

This is a story about a violation of administrative laws. No violence was involved. No guns were fired, no one was stabbed or assaulted, not one person was harmed in any way—other than Yolande and me. The crime she was punished for was simply a violation of government regulations. She did not enter the United States illegally. She did not commit any crime, nor did she cause anyone to suffer any type of physical, emotional or economic loss. However, because of her non-compliance with administrative laws, she was imprisoned for nearly seven weeks and banished from the country.

I'm sure that many people who read this book will feel that we both got exactly what we deserved. We took a chance, practically "thumbed our noses" at the law in their point of view and got caught. "Serves 'em right!" they will probably say. "That's the price you pay for breaking the law!"

I guess everyone is entitled to their viewpoint. But at the same time, I know a lot of people who have broken one or more administrative laws in their life and didn't have to go to jail for it. People who fail to file tax returns, drive without an up to date driver's license, park their cars illegally or commit minor traffic violations never get automatically sent to jail without bail, unless they have seriously harmed someone else or committed the same offense repeatedly. But let someone outside the U.S. stay in this country—just *stay here*—longer than they're supposed to and not only do they get put in jail, they get deported!

My point in writing this book is to attempt to show the inequity of our current immigration policy in the United States through my personal experience. We, as a government, put people in jail whose only offense is coming to or staying in this country in order to make a better life for themselves or their families, even if they haven't done any harm to anyone else, even if they provided useful services. Even if they actually helped other people as caretakers, and actually strengthened our economy by contributing more money into it than they ever take out of it.

Yes, I know there are terrorists in this world who *will* do harm against Americans if they are allowed to come here and stay here unchecked. I am not for one minute saying we should not imprison or deport people who come here to <u>cause harm</u> or <u>commit crimes</u> once they are here. But I *am* saying that people whose only crime is not complying with immigration laws should be given the same opportunity to rectify their transgressions as people who violate tax laws, traffic laws and other administrative regulations—by paying a fine along with any payments due in arrears, and then serving out a probationary period. People who violate tax laws and traffic laws don't automatically get sent to jail! Why should people who come here illegally or stay here illegally be dealt with any more harshly *if they haven't committed any other infractions?* Why shouldn't they be given the same options to make amends for their errors *that violators of other administrative laws are given?*

"Because it's the law!" is the answer I've heard several people give to this question. Yes, it's true that is what our current laws require. But let's face it—there are laws and then there are LAWS. The first kind comes from people and governments. The second kind comes from somewhere else—your own conscience, a sense of right or wrong or perhaps guidance from a higher power. Wherever it comes from, you know when there are laws on the books which conflict with the second, higher level of LAWS. There have been many laws in the past which were morally indefensible, and which some people felt justified in protesting or even violating—helping slaves escape from their owners in the 1800s in America, and hiding Jews from the Nazi government of Germany for example—which were eventually overturned one way or another.

I believe our current immigration laws will be changed one day too. Not without a battle, but once the majority of Americans come to realize just how illogical and inequitable the punishments currently assigned for non-violent, non-harmful violations of immigration law are.

My own parents immigrated to this country from Ireland in the early 1930s under conditions very similar to the ones which motivate illegal immigrants to come to America today. True, they did so legally, but the requirements to emigrate to the U.S. were much more lenient at the time. However, I have no doubt that if there were no other way to do it, they would have done so illegally also.

I hope this book will help people realize that the time for change has already arrived, and that the solution to the current controversy in this area is simply to treat all peaceful, productive human beings with compassion and _common sense_, regardless of their legality in the eyes of the law.

After all, those of us who are not Native Americans are only here in the United States today because many of our great, great ancestors came here "illegally" themselves. And they were the ones who _definitely_ should have been deported if it were possible to do then, because they came here to eventually commit one of the **_biggest crimes_** in history.

They stole a whole **_continent_** away from its rightful owners! And since we're the ones who are now enjoying the benefits of their actions, does that make us illegal too?

Think about it.

HONEYMOON WITH THE BORDER PATROL

Chapter I

"Are you both American citizens?"

It seemed like a simple question. I didn't think there was any way to get it wrong. But I did.

Some people told me afterwards I was just being honest, the way my Irish Catholic parents had taught me to be. Other people, like me, thought I was just plain stupid. I'll let you be the judge.

Yolande and I were sitting in my car, parked approximately 500 feet in front of the entrance to White Sands National Monument. We had left our motel room in Las Cruces a couple of hours earlier and drove roughly 55 miles through the New Mexican desert on Route 70 to see the part of New Mexico that the tourist brochure described as "one of the world's great natural wonders—the glistening white sands of New Mexico. Here, great wave-like dunes of gypsum sand have engulfed 275 square miles of desert and have created the world's largest gypsum dune field", it read. We had one day left on our "honeymoon," (although we preferred to think of it as a mini-vacation) before we had to head back to Long Beach, and we thought 'What the heck?' How often do you get a chance to see 275 square miles of desert engulfed by dunes of gypsum sand?

We drove out over the four lane highway that snaked through the vast desert valley with an occasional huge rock mountain poking its head out of the sand. It was easy to understand why this part of the world was used for nuclear bomb tests over 50 years earlier. Other than a few random trailers parked off on a dirt road here and there, there was virtually nothing there but sand, rock and scrub grass. We looked at the trailers and wondered "Who the hell would ever live out there—and WHY?"

About 100 yards before the brown sign with white letters that read "WHITE SANDS NATIONAL MONUMENT" with an arrow pointing toward the upper right hand corner, a curving row of orange traffic cones channeled the vehicles traveling this lonely stretch of highway down to one lane. I instinctively reached for my wallet to pay whatever fee the National Park Service deemed equitable to allow visitors to view "one of the world's great natural wonders." We came to a stop behind 4 or 5 other cars, obviously waiting for whoever was at the front of the line to pay their fee and pass through.

As we pulled up to the front of the line I noticed something a little strange. There didn't seem to be a booth for the gate keeper to sit in, take in money, and pass out parking permits and brochures. There was just a man in uniform standing on the left hand side of the lane which passed by what looked like a wooden toll booth or guard shack on the right. What was even stranger was the fact that he wasn't wearing the standard U.S. Park Service uniform of a tan shirt, brown pants and brown ranger's hat. Instead, he seemed to be wearing a dark green, almost black shirt and pants and a dark green baseball style hat. As I pulled to a stop and rolled down my window I finally got a good look at him, and I could read the letters printed on his ball cap: "U.S. Border Patrol."

He leaned down to see how many of us were in the car. That's when he asked the question.

"Are you both American citizens?"

For a split second I mentally debated on whether or not to just say yes. He had obviously just asked the same questions of all the cars in front of us and each one of them had passed through after stopping for just a few seconds. If I answered yes I was sure he would simply wave me through to take in the wonders of the white gypsum sands about 500 yards away. All I had to do was say yes and we'd be on our way.

I opened my mouth and to my own astonishment I said, "I am, but she isn't."

He looked at me for a second, and then he looked over at Yolande and said, "Do you have a passport or visa?" She looked back at him, smiled and shook her head. I then started to realize what I had just done.

"We're married," I told him. "We're just here on a little mini-vacation."

"You have a marriage license or a marriage certificate?"

I looked over at Yo. She smiled back and we both shook our heads. Who the hell would think that we'd need a copy of our marriage certificate? We'd just gotten married 8 days earlier in a civil ceremony at the LAX courthouse and we had traveled through 12 states on a car trip across the U.S. a year and a half earlier without any problem, even before we were married. Why would we think we would need a passport, visa or marriage certificate to visit a place just two states away?

"We just got married last week," I told him, like that was going to make any difference. He just kept staring at us through his Border Patrol sunglasses. "Well, I need to see some sort of document that shows that you're married. Do you have any letters or credit card statements? Any bills that have both your names on em?" Nope, we said we didn't have anything like that. He stood there for about 5 seconds and finally said, "Okay, then, pull over here on the side for a couple of minutes. I'll be right back."

For a minute or so, I wondered what the odds were of flooring the gas pedal and speeding off across the desert to out run the Border Patrol cops. Somehow, I didn't think the odds would be very good. Since we were smack dab in one of the most god forsaken parts of the world that you could only get to by one desert highway, excluding horses or helicopters, and that highway didn't have an exit in either direction for about 20 miles, other than the entrance to White Sands, I didn't think we had a very good chance of running. At the same time, I knew that if he walked into that guard shack or into the trailer which I now noticed was parked alongside the road about 100 feet behind us, and entered Yolande's name into the computer, it was pretty much over. I rolled the options around in my head as I pulled over and stopped on the side of the road.

The bottom line was there were no options. We were screwed.

The agent leaned his head into the car and asked Yolande her name and where she was from. She spelled her name out for him and told him she was from Holland.

He said to give him a few minutes and he'd be back. As he walked away, I reached for my cell phone. There was only one thing I could think of that might, just might get us out of this mess: the immigration attorney we had met with about a month before we got married. The only problem was I didn't have her number with me, so I called Cynthia—our roommate, landlord and mutual friend to see if she had it. After all, Cyn was the one who had recommended her to us when we told her we were finally getting married. In fact, she was the one who was more or less responsible for us being together. She had played matchmaker between us after she learned I was trying to escape from my second marriage, with incredibly good results. After that she became our landlord and roommate when she convinced me it would be more economical and simpler for everyone concerned if I moved into the house she and Yo were sharing in Long Beach. But right now, the only thing I cared about was if she had the immigration attorney's number. I dialed my cell phone and prayed she would answer.

Amazingly enough, she was still at home, although by now it was almost 9:00 a.m.! I told her what I needed and why. She understood the urgency in my voice and said to hold on. She found the number I needed and gave it to me over the phone. Then she asked me straight out, "Is Yo going to get deported?" I gave her the only answer I could. "I don't know what's going to happen." We both hung up and I called Catherine Smith, our immigration attorney.

When she answered on the second ring, I started thinking how lucky I was that I was able to contact both Cyn and Catherine on the first try—something that very rarely occurred with either one of them. I was hoping that she would say something like, "Don't worry, it's just a technicality. Give me their number and I'll talk to them and explain everything." After all, she told us once we were married to give her a copy of the marriage certificate and she would begin filling out the forms we would need to get Yo her green card. It might take a few months, but she said once we were married and could prove we had been together for longer than just a couple of months that it would just be a matter of time and money before Yo was a legal resident of the U.S. again. I thought surely she would be able to figure a way out of this, right?

Wrong, wrong, wrong! When she answered the phone, I told her we had a problem we needed help with, and then I told her we had taken a trip to New Mexico.

'WHY WOULD YOU DO THAT?" she screamed.

For a few long seconds I didn't know what to say. To me the question should have been "Why wouldn't you do that?" After all, we had traveled through 12 states together the year before without any problem. We had gone to the Grand Canyon, Yosemite National Park, Mount Rushmore, the Golden Gate Bridge, the Sears Tower and the Badlands National Park without any trouble, and Yo had been living in the U.S. off and on for almost 9 years. Catherine had told us not to get married in Las Vegas like we had planned, in order to have a drive through wedding, but I could not recall her saying anything about not traveling anywhere else. So, although Yo's temporary tourist visa had expired over 4 years earlier, neither one of us had thought we would have anything to worry about as long as we stayed within the U.S. and didn't get on a plane.

"WHY WOULD YOU DO THAT? Catherine screamed at me again. For a second I wanted to let my emotions take over and scream "WHY WOULDN'T WE DO THAT?" right back at her, but I told myself to calm down and remember that this might be the only person who could help us now. "Well, we didn't think there was any reason we couldn't," I said, even though I thought that should have been obvious. "This is EXACTLY what I warned you about. This is EXACTLY what I told you could happen!" she said.

Well, no it's not, I thought. You only told us not to go to Las Vegas. You never said a word about not going anywhere else, I said to myself. At the same time I thought this probably wasn't the best time to try to set the record straight, so I let her rant at me for a few minutes. "I told you, I TOLD YOU about the man from Germany who lost his entire business when he got picked up in New Mexico!" she screamed.

Again, I started thinking "Yeah, you told us about some guy from Germany who started a business in the U.S. without having a green card or a valid visa, but you didn't say he got picked up in New Mexico!" Besides, the thing I remembered most from that story was how stupid it was to start a business in the U.S. if you didn't have a visa or a green card to give you the right to be here. But we didn't do anything like that! We didn't start a business in Yo's name! We didn't cross any international borders! We didn't get on a plane! All we did was try to visit a national monument, which we had already done at least 4 times before in 3 different states! Why would we think this time would be different? And besides, who would have thought there would be a Border Patrol checkpoint 70 miles from the Mexican border?

I let Catherine rant for a few more minutes so she could let me know just how stupid she thought I was. Finally she was able to calm down enough to ask me to tell her exactly what had happened. I gave her all the details while watching the rear view mirror to see if the Border Patrol agent was returning yet. When I finished she let out a big sigh and said, "Okay. I'm going to have to find an attorney out there who can file a change of venue petition, then we're going to have to have her sent back to L.A. and then we're going to have to get her released until she gets a hearing—and then we're going to have to file a petition to have her extradition waived and get a new visa issued, and it's going to take twice as long and cost you three times as much as it would have otherwise." She injected as much disgust into her voice as possible while telling me this, just to make sure I knew what a complete bozo she thought I was. She finished up with another big sigh and then said, "Give me a couple of hours. I'll call you back." "Thank you," I said. I told Yolande what Catherine had said. Then we looked at each other and waited.

After what seemed like at least an hour, the Border Patrol agent came over to the car. He told us that they had entered her information into the computer. According to their records she had overstayed her visa by over 4 years. I told him we knew all that but that we had recently gotten married and had just started working with an attorney to get everything fixed and legalized. He said that was all well and good, but the fact was she had still overstayed her visa and was going to have to go back to Holland.

"When? I asked.

"Today," he said.

"She's going to go back to Holland today?" I asked.

Well, no, he said, but she would probably get sent to the detention center in El Paso and then she would get sent back to Holland from there.

"How long will that take?" I asked. He didn't know. Then he told us someone would let us know when they would be taking her down to the detention center and he walked away.

I looked over at Yo. I couldn't believe this was actually happening. I thought for sure Catherine Smith would find a way to keep her from getting kicked out. Now, for the first time, I was beginning to think that maybe there wasn't any way out and that Yo would actually have to go back to Holland. I started to think that Catherine was right after all. I really was an idiot. Even if she didn't specifically say not to go anywhere except for Las Vegas, why didn't I take the hint and not go <u>anywhere</u> until Yo got her visa renewed? Why didn't I realize that we were just lucky all the other times we went somewhere, and that nobody's lucky forever? Why wasn't <u>Yo</u> ever worried that she might get caught and shipped out? All of these questions kept running through my mind as I looked over at her and thought I might not be able to see her again for a long, long time. And I realized that, at that point, it didn't matter why we never worried about it before. We were going to have to deal with it now. I told her I was sorry.

Of course, Yo acted like it wasn't anything more serious than getting a traffic ticket. "Hey," she said. "It's not your fault. I just took a chance and I got caught. If I have to go back, I have to go back. No use worrying about it."

Somehow the fact that she could take it all in stride didn't make me feel any better. Besides, even if <u>she</u> didn't mind getting sent back to Holland, <u>I</u> did!

See, I'm not usually considered a very romantic type. Before I met Yo I had managed to screw up a marriage that lasted 21 years, and when that one ended I got caught up in a toxic relationship that took me 10 years to get out of. At various times I've been accused of being a total cynic, and a lot of people probably thought I could never fall in love with anyone again, including me. But I did with her—head over heels. She was the most down to earth, honest, sexy, fun-loving, cheerful, unpretentious and easy to get along with woman I had ever met. I was even afraid to tell her how much I loved her at first, because she definitely was not the mushy type and I figured that was probably a sure fire way to get her to disappear on me. And then one night she told me that *she* loved *me*! That was the night I started believing in miracles.

Right then it seemed like a miracle was exactly what we needed. I kept waiting for Catherine to call back. Another hour dragged by. Finally the cell phone rang. This time it was a different attorney. Her name was Margaret Parker. She said she was either a friend or an associate of Catherine's and that Catherine had asked her to take over this case. I really didn't care who took it over as long as somebody was out there trying to keep Yo from getting sent to a "detention center", *aka **jail**!*

She said she was trying to contact some attorneys in the El Paso area, which was where they were telling us Yo would be sent. She also said she would call me back and give me some phone numbers for the El Paso attorneys she could recommend as soon as possible. Even though she didn't have anything new to tell us, she seemed confident that we would be able to get Yo transferred to L.A. within a matter of days, and that she would be released on bail from there until her hearing came up. The most encouraging thing about her was that she wasn't screaming at me like I was a total idiot. She even seemed sympathetic.

After about 2 hours, one of the Border Patrol agents came back to the car and told us we would have to wait in the trailer for the van to come pick Yo up. He escorted us over to a white trailer about 25 feet long and we stepped inside. Inside the trailer was a mini-office with 5 or 6 desks with computers, filing cabinets and about 4 or 5 Border Patrol agents in their dark green uniforms working on their computers or just sitting at their desks bullshitting. Occasionally one of them would go in or out of the trailer to talk to the one standing outside who was asking people in their cars if they were U.S. citizens.

We sat on a padded bench while one of the Border Patrol agents asked Yo a bunch of questions about where she was born, when she last entered the U.S., where she was living in the U.S., etc., etc. As usual, Yo was as co-operative and cheerful as if she was at a bridal shower. She answered all the agent's questions as thoroughly as possible and even threw in a couple of jokes here and there. Eventually, she got to talking to one of the agents who said he had been to Holland, and she asked him how he liked it there, and did he go to the red light district, etc., etc. It seemed to me like she didn't want the poor

Border Patrol agents to feel guilty about trying to kick her out of the country! I didn't think she had to be quite that friendly, but I knew that was her personality. She can't help being friendly to everyone, no matter what the situation. I mean I knew these guys were just doing their job, too, but I didn't think we should be happy about the whole thing.

While we were waiting, we were treated to an amazing display of ineptitude by the agents in the trailer. For some reason, it took a total of 4 different agents to enter Yo's vital information into the computer. They misspelled her first name once, her last name twice, pushed several incorrect keys and had to start over four or five times. They could have been making a video showing how *not* to process a detainee, but I'm pretty sure they were trying to do it correctly. It was a little like watching "The Three Stooges Join The Border Patrol," but it still didn't seem very funny at the time.

After about another hour, an older Border Patrol agent came into the trailer. He was wearing sunglasses, so you couldn't see his eyes. He had a reddish mustache and he had a wad of chewing tobacco stuck in his cheek, and even though you couldn't see his whole face, you could tell he was butt-ugly. From the way the rest of the agents talked to him, it was obvious he was a supervisor or boss of some sort. The agents spent most of the time bullshitting, watching the cars go through the checkpoint outside, and every once in a while bringing someone into the trailer whom they had pulled over and found some kind of illegal substance in his car.

One of the guys they brought in apparently had pot in the car. They took him into another room at the end of the trailer. One of the agents held up the plastic bag with a small amount of pot in the bottom. They were all proud of themselves, saying "Yep, we got one! Had it right in the glove compartment!" Red Mustache held up the bag to see for himself. "Right in the glove compartment, huh?" he asked and gave a little chuckle. Yolande said that amount of pot wouldn't even get you arrested in Holland. Unfortunately we're not in Holland now, I thought.

Sometime around noon, one of the Border Patrol agents said a van was on its way there to take Yolande to El Paso. In the meantime, I got a call on my cell phone from Margaret Parker giving me the names of 3 El Paso attorneys I could call to try to get Yo transferred to L.A. She said that I might not be able to get in touch with any of them today, since it was a Saturday, but I could call and leave a message. She also told me that under no circumstances should Yolande sign anything that waived her right to a hearing.

A little while after I got the call from Margaret, Red Mustache came over to us and told us they were almost ready to send Yo down to El Paso, but that she had to sign some forms first. I read the first form they gave her to sign, and sure enough it stated in black and white that by signing that form she would be waiving her right to a hearing. I immediately told Red Mustache that my attorney had told us not to sign anything like that. He said Yolande didn't have a choice because they had found out the visa she came to the U.S. on specifically stated that she could not change her immigration status while she was still in the U.S.—she would have to go back to Holland in order to apply for a new visa. I told him I still didn't want her to sign that form and wanted to call my attorney to discuss it with her. He said I could go ahead and call, but it wouldn't do any good. One way or another she would have to go to El Paso and she wouldn't be able to get a hearing because of the visa she had signed before she came here.

I called Margaret and told her what was going on. At first she said, "See, that's the trouble with Border Patrol agents. They think they know the law and they don't. I know the visa he's talking about, and even though it says on there that she can't change her status while she's still in the U.S., there have been court cases that have upheld a person's right to change their status if they had married a U.S. citizen after they arrived here." I told her that was good news but what were we supposed to do now? I had three Border Patrol agents staring at me and telling me she had to sign that form acknowledging that she had overstayed her visa and had no right to a hearing.

After a few seconds, Margaret changed her mind and said "You know what? Let her go ahead and sign it. It's not going to matter either way. We can file a motion to get her a change of venue to L.A. and the judges here know the law better than the Border Patrol guys, so she'll still be able to get a hearing." I asked her if she was sure that would work, and she said yes, that it wouldn't be a big deal. So I told Yo it was okay to sign.

After she did, Red Mustache said to me, "You know I hate to see people pay attorneys all this money for something like this because the visa that your wife signed makes it impossible for her to have a hearing. The only thing she can do at this point is to go back to Holland and reapply from there. That's the only thing she can do, I don't care what any attorney says." I didn't want to believe it at the time, but for all practical purposes, old Red was right.

After we'd been sitting in the trailer for about 2 hours one of the Border Patrol agents told me the van would be there soon, and I had to leave the trailer. I asked if I could see Yo before she had to leave and Red Mustache said he would come get me before she had to go. I asked him what she could take with her and he said one change of clothes and a jacket, so I went out to get her those things from the car. I came back in, gave her her things and kissed her. Then she cheerfully went off to the other room in the trailer like she was on her way to Disneyland.

I waited in the car for at least another hour, watching for the Border Patrol van. Finally I saw Yolande and Red Mustache come out of the trailer. He came up to the car and told me that there was some problem with getting the van up from El Paso, so they were going to drive her down to the detention center themselves. He also gave me the address there if I wanted to go down to visit her. I asked him what the visiting hours were and he said he didn't know. Yolande came over to get some more underwear and something else out of the car. She still acted like she was just going to take a bus downtown and be right back. I gave her a kiss and told her I loved her, and she said "ik hou van jau," which is "I love you" in Dutch.

Red Mustache held out his hand to me and said "I'm sorry, but there's really nothing else we can do because of the visa she signed. This is the only option we have." No it's not, I thought. You could just let her go and pretend that none of this ever happened. Pretend I just said yes when the other guy asked me if we were both U.S. citizens. Pretend we had stayed put in California until Yo got her new visa and avoided this whole nightmare. But then I realized none of that was going to happen, so I just shook Red's hand and said thanks.

"Okay then", he said. "That should take care of it." Then he turned and started walking away, leaving Yolande standing next to me at the car. After he took a few steps he turned around and said to her "Wait a minute! You've got to come with me!" Of course Yolande laughed at this and started walking to the Border Patrol car. I admit I even had to laugh at that one. But then I caught myself and thought, "What the hell am I laughing about?"

I got in the car and realized that I hadn't gone to the bathroom during this whole episode and now I really had to. So I drove up the road a few yards to the first exit—the entrance to White Sands National Monument! I went inside to the bathroom and took a quick look around behind the visitors' center before I went back to the car. Yep, there were big white sand dunes back there alright. They actually looked like big hills of snow, sitting right in the middle of the desert! They probably would have been a lot of fun to go climb on and take pictures of, if Yo was still with me.

But right then I wished I'd never heard of the place. I got in my car and started driving to El Paso.

WELCOME TO EL PASO

Chapter II

I kept looking for the Border Patrol car, but I couldn't find it on the highway. I kept thinking they must have gotten in the car and immediately headed south for El Paso while I stopped for 5 minutes to take a whiz at the White Sands monument. I kept thinking I'd eventually catch up to them but I didn't. When I crossed the Texas border I looked for the Welcome Center sign. As soon as I saw it I pulled in to get a map so I could find the detention center in El Paso.

The lady at the counter was trying to be as helpful as possible. She was a cheerful Texas lady in her mid fifties who just seemed to love her job answering questions and giving directions to the tourists who passed through the Welcome Center. She gave me the tourist map and showed me how to get to El Paso from where we were. I asked her if she knew how to get to the address that Red Mustache gave me.

She looked a little puzzled.

"I'm not sure I know exactly where that is, honey. Is it a business or a residence?"

I told her it was neither. It was a U.S. Immigration detention center.

She actually hid her surprise very well, but you could tell by the way she was acting so businesslike about it, that she hadn't expected me to say that. She did a good job of keeping it under wraps, however, and tried to show me on the map where she thought it was, and the best way to get there. I thanked her for her help and got back in the car to go find El Paso in the late afternoon sun.

☙

I had met Yolande over 2 and a half years earlier when I auditioned for a little murder mystery dinner theater show. I had been bouncing around in community theater and "Equity Waiver" shows for over 20 years and had been trying to get somewhere with an acting career in Southern California for the last 9 years when I met her. Obviously I hadn't had much luck at that point, since I was still auditioning for shows like "Cincinnati Smith and the Tomb of Doom." Actually, I knew it would be hokey, but that was okay. I had been in a murder mystery show before and I knew that that was the idea, what the audiences wanted. In fact, the hokier it was the more the audiences loved it. Besides, according to the ad in Back Stage West, they were actually going to be <u>paying</u> the actors who got cast in this show.

That was the main reason I was trying out for it. My wife would have a fit whenever I took a part in a play or low budget film that didn't pay anything—and most of the parts I could get cast in didn't. Then I would have to listen to her complain and interrogate me about why I wanted to spend all that time rehearsing and performing for free? How could they ask people to do so much work for nothing? Because they can, I tried to tell her. Because most actors are like me—they're so desperate to get a part, any part, that they'll do it for free if they have to. As long as they think they can get even the slightest exposure from it, they'll *gladly* do it for nothing. In fact, they'll even spend their <u>own</u> money if they have to, and most of the time they have to. No, it's definitely not fair, I used to tell her, but unfortunately, that's just the way it is 90 % of the time. So when I saw a chance to audition for a part that paid, I was definitely interested.

The audition was held in a town about 5 miles from Long Beach at a place that was called the West End Theater. I walked into the theater and started looking for a sign in sheet. There were actually two shows that were having auditions there that evening—the murder mystery show and the classic musical comedy "The Fantasticks." I wasn't sure if they were offering any pay for "The Fantasticks," but I had been in that show years ago, when I was first starting out in community theater and I thought it would be fun to do it again, possibly playing another part. I entered the building and was walking through the main hallway looking for a sign for "The Fantasticks" or "Cincinnati Smith." I spotted a sign with an arrow pointing to the left that said "The Fantasticks" and started to walk that way.

Before I could take two steps I heard someone with just a hint of a European accent clearing their throat and saying "Hello? Are you here for the auditions?" I turned around and saw a short, pretty, friendly looking woman in her early thirties (I thought), with short, curly reddish-brown hair standing at the other end of the hall. "Yes," I said. "For Cincinnati Smith?" she asked. "Well, I was going to audition for 'The Fantasticks' *and* 'Cincinnati Smith'," I told her.

"Oh," she said. She sounded a little disappointed. "Can I do that?" I asked. She shrugged her shoulders and gave me her best "I *GUESS* so" look, but she said "Sure!" "Okay, then I'll see you after I get done in there," I said pointing in the same direction as the arrow on the audition sign.

I went in for the "Fantasticks" audition. It must not have been very memorable, because I can't remember anything about it. As soon as that was over I walked down the hall and sat down to wait my turn to audition for "Cincinnati Smith." While I was sitting there, the woman I had met in the hallway came back one more time to tell all the actors what the pay arrangements would be (one dollar for every audience member at each show!). Again, I noticed some kind of accent, but I wasn't sure what it was. I heard one of the other actors asking where the "Dutch lady" had gone, so I assumed that had to be her. At some point she either introduced herself or someone else told me her name. It was Yolande.

I auditioned for the part of Cincinnati Smith himself, using my best Australian accent, since the sides I had been given to read indicated that was the character's nationality. Cynthia, the woman who wrote the script and was running the audition, gave me the usual "thank you" and said she would be calling the people who would be cast by the following day.

The next day Cynthia called and said I had the "worst Australian accent she had ever heard in her life"—but gave me the part anyway! This would be the first of several statements and comments that Cynthia would make to me that I never quite understood. But the truth was I was always happy to get cast in a part—especially since I usually <u>didn't</u>. My success rate was well below 10 % when you considered all the film and commercial rehearsals I did, as well as for stage shows, so getting cast in anything was always an ego booster for me.

Over the next month or so we had auditions at Cynthia's house in Long Beach. Although I never said anything about it, it was obvious to me that some of the people in the cast were actually *very* untalented as actors. I didn't think of myself as a Robert De Niro or a Laurence Olivier, but the fact was that some of them were just pretty lousy compared to other people I had worked with. On top of that, a few of them were "musical theater" actors, which I soon found out were a very different breed of actor in California.

I hadn't performed in very many musicals, but the community theater shows I did back in Illinois were as good, if not better, than many professionally staged shows I have seen. "Damn Yankees" and "The Fantasticks" were performed at Lewis University in Lockport, Illinois back in the late 70s, and the people who were cast in those shows with me were, for the most part, dedicated, talented performers. More importantly, they usually acted like <u>normal</u> people when they weren't performing. This was not to be the case with my fellow actors in "Cincinnati Smith."

The "musical theater" actors who were cast in the Cincinnati Smith show all had one thing in common—they were in love with the sound of their own voices. They had the annoying habit of bursting into song at the most unexpected times—while you were talking to someone during a rehearsal break or at a restaurant during an after show cast party, for example—and then acting like they were doing you a favor by allowing you to listen to them.

I was definitely not impressed by these fellow cast members who seemed to take every opportunity to try to "show off" their wonderful voices for the rest of the world during our rehearsals. In fact, I thought they were downright annoying. But I thought I was the only one who felt that way.

After spending 4 or 5 rehearsals at Cynthia's house and being "treated" to several impromptu renditions of songs that some of the cast had sung, or liked, from other musical shows they had been in, I finally had to make a comment. There were 6 or 7 of us standing in Cynthia's kitchen, including

Cynthia and Yolande, munching on some of the snacks she usually provided at rehearsals. Cynthia was with the cast during every rehearsal, directing and explaining the script she had written. However, Yolande was the costume designer and prop manager for the show, and aside from taking measurements during one of the early rehearsals, she rarely had anything to do with the cast. In fact she deliberately stayed out of sight for most of the rehearsals.

However, she happened to be in the kitchen with the rest of us during this particular break. One or more of the other cast members decided that this was a good time to serenade everyone with yet another sample of her *lovely* voice. I finally felt compelled to mutter something like "It's like fingernails on a blackboard" while I walked out of the kitchen to escape the concert, and both Cynthia and Yolande started laughing and nodding as they walked out with me.

"You don't like that either?" I asked them. "NO!" Cynthia said. "Believe me, we are *NOT* musical theater people!" I found that a little hard to believe since they had both just stood by listening during each of the previous "concerts," as far as I could remember. However, Cynthia and Yo assured me that they actually hated having to listen to the other cast members' "gifts" as much as I did. That was the first time I remember actually talking to Yo.

I had never paid much attention to her before, because even though I thought she was cute and pretty, she always tried to hide out while rehearsals were going on. She had been working on costumes and props for Cynthia's shows for years and by that time she was extremely tired of listening to the actors babbling out a never ending supply of self-centered dialogues and their frequent musical outbursts. Her solution was to stay in the back of the house, out of sight, until the rehearsals were finally over. Now that I had found someone who shared my disgust with the self-centeredness of the musical theater actors, however, I began talking to her much more often.

Slowly, over the course of the "Cincinnati Smith" show and the following one, which I was also cast in, I became aware that there seemed to be some attraction between us. It started when someone was needed to give Yo a ride to one of her pet-sitting jobs after one of the shows or a rehearsal. Since I now enjoyed talking to her and also trashing the other "musical theater" actors, I usually volunteered. I found her very likable and she actually seemed interested in me, which was very good for the old ego, I must admit.

As the rides got to be more frequent, and the attraction started to become stronger, I began to feel guilty. I was still married, although by this time there really wasn't any love left in the marriage and I knew it was just a matter of time before we divorced. My wife and I were simply going through the motions because we didn't know what else to do.

We had been together almost 10 years, been married for 5, and during all that time, I'll bet we never went longer than 3 days without a major fight. Not only did we have a lot of fights, but the fights we had were as mean and nasty as anything you can imagine. Lately they had gotten pretty violent as well. We had lots of problems, which I will not go into detail about here, but I think it's fair to say that we were both equally guilty for making the other one miserable and for prolonging the agony as long as we did.

Two things we both had in common were a stubborn streak and a bad, bad temper. I had gone through periods in my past in which I had some problems with anger management before we were together, but after we got married it got worse than ever. Within a year, we got into such major physical battles that the neighbors called the police on us 3 times—and I even called them myself once. We both said an awful lot of mean and hurtful things to each other, which led to the physical fights, and I am definitely not proud of my behavior during those years. I literally tried to leave several times, but every time I came back to get more clothes after four or five days at a motel, she would make me feel so guilty that I'd agree to try and start all over again. But it always went back to the way it was before within a week.

I hated having to stay with her, but didn't know anyone that would let me stay with them until I could find a place of my own. I didn't have any family to stay with. I had been an only child and both my parents had passed away years ago. In addition, all of my friends in California were husbands or boyfriends to women who were friends with my wife. To top it all off, my wife had told me that if I ever left for good, she would never allow me back in the house to get the rest of my clothes and possessions. In other words, if I left, I had to take everything I wanted to keep with me because I would never be allowed back in. But if she saw me trying to pack my things and leave she would get furious and we would have another knock-down drag out brawl! So neither one of us could stand living with the other, but at the same time I couldn't find a way to leave without losing almost everything I owned. I was in Hell.

We had about 6 or 7 performances of "Cincinnati Smith" at a hotel restaurant in Long Beach, and even though it was incredibly hokey and we had some truly horrible actors in it, the audiences all seemed to enjoy it. I came to realize that for this type of dinner theater, the show didn't have to be all that good. The scripts were actually pretty good, and the audience could logically guess who the murderers in the shows were if they really paid attention, but nobody really cared if the actors were any good. They were just there to provide a diversion during a dinner out as far as the audience was concerned. So even if the actors forgot half their lines, which sometimes happened, the audience really didn't mind. They were there to enjoy the novelty of it all. And even though we never got a lot of people to come to our shows, the ones that did actually seemed to enjoy them.

After Cincinnati Smith, Cynthia wrote another dinner show called "A Royal Wedding" that she asked me to be in. Even though the turnout for Cincinnati Smith had been disappointing, and we didn't get paid very much as a result, I didn't mind being in another show with Cynthia as the director and Yo as the costumer. I was working a number of different sales type jobs at the time because I desperately wanted to find a way to make a living doing something besides Accounting, (which was my primary occupation for nearly 25 years), so my schedule was generally pretty flexible. Besides, I was always glad to find something that would get me out of the house and away from my wife for a while.

We did about 4 or 5 performances of "A Royal Wedding," and after the final show we had planned to go to a local lounge for our closing night cast party. As we were getting ready to leave Cynthia made up some excuse about not being able to go to the party and asked me if I could give Yo a ride home afterward. I wondered if they both really thought I didn't know that this was a set up designed to get me and Yolande alone together one last time. But I actually didn't mind being with her anyway, so I just played dumb and said okay.

We went to a nearby pub and sang karaoke songs (of course, since most of the people there were the "musical theater" actors). By this time, I knew Yo was definitely interested in me. Since I thought this might be the last night I would ever see her, I couldn't resist giving in and giving her a good, long kiss to remember me by when I dropped her off. I half expected her to be shocked, maybe even slap me, but she didn't. She kissed back.

I kissed her back more. She kissed back harder. Before I knew it, things were becoming a lot more serious than I had planned. Without going into too much detail, I have to say I was very, um, _surprised_ at her reaction. After that, I never thought of her as a quiet, shy little woman again.

After that night, I felt like I had to see her again. She started calling me while I was working on my sales jobs, so I knew she felt the same way. I had tried out for, and got cast in a play at a theater in Long Beach not far from Cynthia's house, which is where Yo lived as her roommate. Even though I still felt terribly guilty, I couldn't resist the opportunity to go see her after our rehearsals or shows at least once a week.

This went on for 5 or 6 weeks. At first I told myself I would only see her a few times and then it would be over. But every time I left her I wanted to see her again.

Finally I realized that I would have to find a way to leave my wife. Even though we slept in separate beds now, and there was virtually nothing even close to romance in our marriage, I still felt like I couldn't leave until I had someplace to put all my clothes and possessions that I would have to take with me. However, Cynthia was well aware of the growing romance between Yo and me, especially since she had been instrumental in making sure we found a way to finally get together. She also knew that I wanted to eventually divorce my wife, and seeing an opportunity to make both Yo and me happy, she gave me the best Christmas present I ever got. She told me I could bring all my clothes and belongings to her house and stay there until I could find a place of my own.

I waited until well after year end, partly for my convenience, but mostly because I really thought it would be less traumatic to wait until after the holidays to make my move. I waited until my wife was out of the house one night in February and moved my stuff out while she was gone. Even though we had made each other miserable for almost 10 years, and I knew it was what I had to do, I still felt terrible about it. I left her a note and a long, long message on the answering machine to tell her that this time it was for good. Then I kissed and hugged my two beautiful Black Labradors who had been curiously watching me load up a rented van with clothes and keepsakes for well over an hour. It was the one of the hardest things, maybe even **the** hardest thing I've ever had to do in my life, but I knew I would never get out any other way. I also knew if we stayed together, one or both of us would end up dead or in prison one day. So I left.

I stayed at Cyn's for a couple of weeks until I could get my own apartment and then I moved out. My wife left several messages asking me to call her after I left. I waited for a couple of days for everything to cool down and called her from my office at work. Within minutes we were screaming at each other over the phone. Nothing had changed at all. I ended up hanging up on her and trying to communicate via email, but most of the time that was just a series of hate mails back and forth.

After about a week, she called and asked me to meet her for lunch so we could talk about what had happened. I told her I would meet with her but nothing would change. She said that everything would be different if I came back, but I knew it wouldn't. Besides, I told her, I had someone in my life now that I honestly believed I had a chance to be happy with for a long time, and I wasn't about to give up that chance. I told her that we had spent 10 years together trying to make our relationship work and we never even came close. It was definitely past time for both of us to move on, but I knew she wouldn't be able to see it. But even if she couldn't, I could—so I told her I was sorry, but this was the end for us.

We eventually got divorced, but unfortunately it was not an amicable parting. It took nearly 2 years to get everything settled. Time eventually healed most of the scars and we can now talk to each other without bitterness, but it was a long, *long*, painful process. We truly never should have gotten together in the first place. Why we did is something I still don't know the answer to. Maybe some day some psychologist will be able to explain it to me.

During this time Yolande and I were with each other at least 4 days out of every week. I knew she was definitely not the mushy type, so even though I felt I had found the perfect woman for me, I tried really hard not to tell her. Even though I loved her for her honesty, her practicality, her generosity and her straight forward, unashamed sexuality, I didn't dare tell her because I thought that was the one thing that would make her leave. Incredibly enough, after about 2 or 3 months of being together, she was the one who told me she loved ***me!***

I felt like one of the living again! After almost 10 years of being angry and depressed most of the time, now I was happy and excited. It was just like how you were supposed to feel when you were in love. And this was the first time I felt that way in a <u>long</u> time.

After my divorce got finalized we immediately started making plans to get married. However, neither one of us wanted a big, expensive wedding (she was definitely more practical than any other woman I ever knew!), so we planned on going to Las Vegas for a "drive through" wedding. Yolande reasoned that Las Vegas was the only place in the world where you could do this, so that's how she wanted to get married!

We were only getting married to enable her to get a new visa and a green card anyway. Neither one of us believed that a marriage certificate made two people any more or less in love, or any more or less committed to the other one. We believed that if two people love each other, then they would stay together no matter what. If they didn't love each other, they wouldn't, no matter how many pieces of paper they have. I was living proof of that, just like anyone else who's gotten divorced.

In other words, we looked at the marriage certificate as a legal document, nothing more, nothing less. It was the legal document which would allow us to get Yolande's visa renewed and eventually allow us to travel anywhere in the world together without worrying about legalities. However, after Catherine Smith warned us about potential Border Patrol checkpoints outside of Vegas, we ruled out the drive through wedding.

Neither one of us remembered hearing her say anything about not going anywhere else…

I got to the detention center in El Paso about 4:30 in the afternoon. I drove up to the guard shack and asked the Border Patrol agent when visiting hours were. He said tomorrow, Sunday from 12 to 3, and then again on Friday at the same times. Then I asked him how long the detainees were usually kept there before they were released. Oh, gosh, he said, he didn't know for sure, but he thought they were usually there a minimum of 30 days.

"Thirty days!" I thought to myself. "Bullshit!"

I turned my car around and started heading out of the parking lot to the street. "Ain't no way in hell they're keeping Yo in there for 30 days!" I thought. I'll get hold of one of those lawyers on Monday morning and we'll get this whole damn thing straightened out in a hurry. Thirty days, my ass! I'm an American citizen! They're not going to do this to my wife! I'll get her sent back to L.A. and then we'll just have to go from there, like Margaret Parker said.

I pulled out of the detention center onto the street and started looking for a cheap motel in downtown El Paso.

TALES FROM THE DETENTION CENTER

Chapter III

I found a relatively cheap motel on the south side of town that night. While I was there, Catherine Smith called me again to follow up on what had happened after Margaret called me. I told her how she had given me the names and numbers of 3 attorneys in El Paso, whom I had called but could only leave voice mail messages for. Then she launched into another lecture about how this was <u>exactly</u> what she had told me could happen, and why did I ever take a trip to New Mexico? By this time, I had had enough. I told her that the only thing I had remembered her telling us, as far as places not to go was Las Vegas. Yes, I remembered her telling us about the man from Germany who started a business in the U.S. without a valid visa, and ended up losing everything he owned, but I thought she was telling us that to warn us not to start a business in Yolande's name, and I *NEVER* heard her say anything about not going anywhere else! If she had told us that, I <u>wouldn't</u> have gone anywhere, but the only thing I remember her saying was to stay away from Vegas! I ended by telling her that we had told Cynthia where we were going, and she didn't seem to think there was anything to worry about, and Yolande obviously wasn't concerned, so I wasn't the only one who didn't see anything wrong with taking a trip to New Mexico!

I finally convinced her that when she told us that Yolande would need a renewed visa and a green card to travel safely, that we thought she was talking about *air* travel, since we had already traveled so extensively by car, and that we weren't simply ignoring her advice. She finally seemed to understand and calmed down. She ended the call by telling me to keep in touch and let her know how things worked out.

The next morning, I drove to the local K-Mart to buy some books and magazines to bring to Yo when I went to visit her at the detention center. I had breakfast at the local Denny's and drove around El Paso to try to find a cheaper motel to reserve a room for that night, since I knew I wouldn't be leaving until I talked to one of the three lawyers I had called. Finally, at about 11:45 a.m. I drove to the detention center and told them I was there to see my wife who had been picked up by the Border Patrol the day before. The guard at the entrance gate didn't seem to need anything more than that and raised the gate to let me in.

The first thing that told me the detention center was really nothing more than a prison was the fact that I had to wait outside in a line of people who were also there to visit someone inside, and we could only go inside one person at a time. A guard on the other side of the glass doors waved in the people in line, one by one, in 5 or 6 minute intervals until he got to me. Once I got inside I stood in another line in front of a cheap, modern looking desk that a heavy set woman in the official Immigration Service uniform sat behind, asking visitors to sign the register and inspecting everything they brought in with them.

When I got to the front of the line, I was told by the receptionist that I would have to leave the books and magazines in the car. The only way any books or magazines could arrive at the detention center was via the U.S. mail. Okay, I said. I went out and put the books and magazines I had planned to give to Yo in the car. Then I stood in line to get inside again.

Once I was in, I had to sign a register and tell them the name of the detainee I was there to see. When I told them the name was Wassenberg, they had to repeat it a few times to make sure they had heard it right. "Wass-en-berg?" they asked. "Right", I told them. They looked as though they didn't expect to hear a name that sounded so Germanic for anyone staying there. As I looked around the waiting room at the other visitors sitting in plastic chairs, it was obvious that most of the detainees there probably had names more like Sanchez, Lopez or Garcia than Wassenberg.

She told me to put the contents of my pockets into a plastic tub and a male guard wearing the same uniform as the woman behind the desk took the tub and put my wallet, change and keys into a gray, foot square locker stacked against one of the walls. Then he gave me the locker key and told me I could open it when I left. I said thank you and went to sit on one of the plastic chairs until they called Yolande's name.

After about 20 minutes, a guard opened the gray metal door with a window panel at the rear of the waiting area and called out "Wassenberg!" I walked through the door and then let the guard run his hand held metal detector up and down the front, rear and sides of my body. When he was satisfied that I didn't have anything metal tucked away inside my clothes, he let me pass down the corridor. "Third window", another heavy set female guard who was sitting at a small desk in the corridor said to me. "What do they feed these people?" I wondered as I walked past her.

I walked down the corridor a few feet to a space where there was a small cubicle recessed into the wall with a large picture window in front of it. In front of the window was a plastic chair and on the wall to the right was a phone. I sat down on the chair and waited.

Within a few minutes Yo appeared on the opposite side of the window and sat down. She was wearing a blue denim blouse and pants. Even though she now looked like, and actually <u>was</u> a federal prisoner, she still greeted me with a big grin as she sat on the other side of the window. Since the glass was too thick to talk through, we had no choice but to pick up the phones on either side of the wall, silly as it seemed.

"How are you?" I asked. It really sounded stupid once I said it, but I didn't know what else to say. "Okay" was the predictable response. I then asked her what time she had gotten there yesterday, and to my surprise she said about midnight! I asked her how in the world it could have taken that long, since I left her when she was getting in the car with Red Mustache around 3:00 p.m. in the afternoon, and I went into the White Sands visitor's center to pee before I drove to El Paso.

She said that it was a comedy of errors. Apparently, the van that was coming to get her had to go to another Border Patrol station at Alamogordo first, which was a nearby town approximately 40 miles in the other direction. It took about an hour to get there and then they waited until after 10:00 p.m. for another detainee to arrive from some other checkpoint. Once they got to El Paso they had to stop at the gate and exchange paperwork, and by the time they finally got out of the van and walked into the detention center it was after 12:00 p.m.

After she arrived, Yo was put in a cell for about an hour. Then she was brought into the main office for another round of questions about how long she had been in the U.S., why she had overstayed her visa, etc., etc. She answered all the questions and was returned to her cell. Then, about an hour later, they brought her out of the cell into the main office and asked the same questions *AGAIN*!

After answering the agents' questions a second time, she was taken back to the holding cell. From approximately 1:00 a.m. until 4:00 a.m. she was "treated" to the sound of music being played at a ridiculously high volume from a guard's radio. Obviously they wanted to make sure she didn't fall asleep too soon!

Finally after enduring approximately three hours of sound torture, they let her take a shower and gave her her prison clothes. They also gave her a thin blanket to cover herself with and told her she could sleep on the floor until they could arrange to have her transferred to a bed in one of the barracks. I asked her what time she finally got transferred into the barracks. She laughed and said "About 7 o'clock this morning."

7 o'clock! I couldn't believe it! I had slept in a nice, comfortable motel bed and was already starting on my breakfast by the time she was just getting to sleep in a bed! This was already 10 times worse than I thought it could be! And she was laughing about it! I often wondered how she could laugh about things like that. I would be ready to rip somebody's head off if it was me!

Even though I was upset, she said not to say anything. She told me that that she couldn't help but laugh at all the things that went on there, but she kept her voice low when she said it and she didn't want to go into any detail. I thought for a few minutes that she was being overly cautious, but then I realized we were 12 inches away from each other, talking to each other via telephones, looking at each other through a glass window, and she had just endured over 18 hours of being picked up, transported and processed before she was allowed to sleep on a concrete floor—and all because she had stayed in this country longer than she should have.

I understood why the government had laws to limit the number of outsiders allowed into the country at any given point in time. I also understood why, after 9/11, that enforcing immigration laws was a high priority to many Americans. But I could not understand why the enforcement had to be done with such blatant disregard for human decency.

She hadn't committed any crimes, she hadn't taken anyone's job away from them, she hadn't received any public services from any state or federal government. Instead, she had provided needed services to a handicapped person and usually received just food and lodging for all the other services she provided—sometimes not even that. Yet, here she was being treated, for all practical purposes, like an escaped animal—thrown into a cage and left there until the powers that be could find the time to deal with her.

Yes, I understood that, bottom line, we had to admit it was her own fault—but I still felt that the "Big Brother" treatment she was receiving was really going a bit overboard. And after reading about all the abuses that took place at Abu Ghraib and Guantanamo Bay, it didn't take a lot of imagination to believe that the people in charge might <u>not</u> be too concerned with the human rights of the people being detained there. After all, they weren't supposed to be here to begin with, right? I decided she had every right to be cautious and even a little bit fearful. This place was definitely not intended to make you feel relaxed and worry free.

We made small talk for a little while longer and then I suddenly found out that the visiting "hours" were limited to 15 minutes per visitor! One of the female guards came by on Yolande's side of the glass and said "OK, five more minutes." "Five minutes?" I asked her. "Yep, five minutes. Visitations only last 15 minutes!"

We didn't really have that much to say anyway. I mean what could you say beyond, "Did you get any sleep?" and she had already told me about the nightmare she went through getting processed the night before. Besides, it didn't seem wise to say too much about the conditions, or the competence of the guards, given that the people being held there weren't American citizens and their well being didn't seem to be of the highest priority. So we basically said "I love you" and I asked her to call me when she could. (She had told me that I wouldn't be able to call her on the phone. She could call me, but only when she could buy a phone card from a vending machine there, and all her calls were subject to monitoring.) I told her we should press our palms together against the window like they did in the movies, but she thought that was way too hokey. So we just smiled at each other and said "Houdoe."

I went back to the motel and waited to see if I would get a call from one of the El Paso attorneys by the next morning.

THE GOOD OLD BOY ATTORNEY

Chapter IV

*L*ater that evening, I got a call from Leroy Durkin in my motel room. That's not his real name, because knowing attorneys, if he ever reads this, he may try to sue me, even though I'm not saying anything that isn't true. But knowing how attorneys can find ways to create lawsuits out of minor incidents, I wouldn't put it past him to try to punish me for telling the truth about him.

He was the first of the 3 El Paso attorneys that I had left a message with to return my call. I briefly told him the story about how Yo had gotten picked up by the Border Patrol on Saturday and finally transferred into the detention center early the next morning, and that Margaret Parker had given me his name and number to help us get Yo transferred back to L.A., etc. He said we had better take first things first, and that he would have to find out the name of the supervisor of the guards who were in charge of her building, and THEN, we would have to find out if she was even going to get a hearing! I told him that Margaret Parker had indicated on the phone to me that she seemed to think it could be done, and he responded by saying that, well, he knew a lot of people thought that things which worked in other jurisdictions would work the same way here, too, but that this was <u>El Paso</u>, and things worked a little differently down here!

I told him that all I knew was what Margaret Parker had told me on the phone, and I would appreciate it if he would call her in the morning to get her take on the situation. He assured me he would, but he cautioned me again that, although he was sure she was a good attorney, he said that any attorney practicing in southern California, no matter how good she was, couldn't possibly know what the situation was like dealing with the Immigration Service in El Paso. He said, "You've got to understand, you're dealing with the *Gestapo* down here. They do things their own way."

Durkin said that all immigration arrests used to be handled by the Border Patrol as part of the Immigration Department. Then they felt that they had to separate the Border Patrol from immigration enforcement, so they came up with a new agency—ICE, which stands for Immigration and Customs Enforcement, and it was a whole different ballgame now. Immigration is such a hot political issue right now, he told me, that the government created ICE specifically to toughen up immigration law enforcement. "ICE is a whole different animal from the Border Patrol", he said, "and they play by their own rules."

I didn't know if he was really giving me the inside scoop on how things really worked within Immigration Services, or if he was just trying to give me his cop outs in advance, before he actually did anything. Well, was he willing to try to do what Margaret Parker recommended, I asked? Oh, sure, sure, he said, he just wanted to let me know what we were going to have to deal with. That's your job, not mine, I thought, but again, I felt like the only course of action available right now was to hope that Durkin could do what Margaret had recommended the day before. Since she had recommended him, I could only hope that he knew what he was talking about. In any event, he gave me the address to his office in downtown El Paso, and I agreed to meet him there the next day at 10:00 a.m.

The next day I drove to downtown El Paso to find Durkin's office, based on the directions he had given me the night before. I got off Interstate 10 at the exit he told me to use and drove around for a few blocks to try to find a place to park. Durkin hadn't told me that his office was located in one of the seedier parts of El Paso, although after having spent a couple of days there already, I could honestly say that none of it was what you'd call pretty. I was hoping I would be able to find a parking spot on one of the busier downtown streets instead of paying 8 or 9 dollars to park in one of the crummy, trash strewn asphalt parking lots in the area, but no such luck. Even if I had found an open space, I realized I probably didn't have enough change on me to feed the meter, and not enough time to go get change and come back. So I drove into a local pay lot and walked the 3 blocks to Durkin's office.

As I got off the elevator on the 3rd floor, I began to get a bad feeling about the whole situation. The corridor outside Durkin's office was relatively narrow, with dingy looking off white walls and shabby, old red maroon carpeting. The whole place seemed to yell out "Cheesy!" But still, this was El Paso, not Chicago, Boston or L.A., I tried to remind myself.

I heard someone talking behind the door to Durkin's office. It was actually a few minutes past 10, so I knocked on the door just to let him know I was there. "Just a minute", a voice called out. I waited for 2 or 3 minutes and the door opened. Durkin was standing in the doorway wearing a long sleeved shirt and tie. He was in his mid to late 50s with thinning brown hair and a serious look on his face. "Ah'm sorry, ah'm in the middle of a phone call right now. Could you just have a seat in the hall and I'll be with you in a few minutes?" he asked. What was I going to do, say no?

I sat in the hallway while Durkin finished his call and wondered if I should go any further with him. If his office was any indication of his success as an attorney, it didn't fill me with confidence. Then again, I reminded myself, he was an immigration attorney, working in El Paso, Texas, and the vast majority of his clients were probably relatively poor Mexicans who needed someone to fight for them and couldn't afford to pay what most attorneys would charge for their services. I told myself that maybe he was a good guy trying to fight for the little guy. At least that was the most optimistic way of looking at it that I could think of at the time, so that's how I chose to view it.

After a few minutes, Durkin finished his call, came out into the hallway where I was sitting and invited me into his office. Sitting in a chair in his tiny office once again made me think that he was either a do-gooder attorney who didn't have a big fancy office because he was working for the poor illegal immigrants who couldn't get anyone else to try to help them, or he was simply not one of the best lawyers to have representing you. Again, since he had been recommended by Margaret Parker, who had been recommended by Catherine Smith, I chose to believe the former instead of the latter.

He told me basically the same story that he had told me on the phone the evening before—namely that he would have to find the supervisor in charge of the guards for Yolande's building, try to get a copy of the charges and find out when and <u>IF</u> she was going to have a hearing. He didn't sound nearly as confident as Margaret Parker had sounded, so I asked him if he had talked to her. He said he had, and that he would certainly try to file a motion to have Yolande transferred to L.A. and have her released on bail, but <u>first</u> he had to get a copy of the charges and <u>then</u> he had to find out if she could have a hearing.

He said he didn't want to discourage me, but a lot of times, based on what kind of visa the person had signed, they couldn't even get a hearing if it was the type of visa that would not allow them to change their immigration status while they were still in the U.S. This all started sounding very similar to what Red Mustache had told me, and I started hoping Margaret Parker knew what she was talking about and these guys didn't. In any event, I didn't know what else to do, so I gave him a check for the $500 fee he said he would need to start working on the case. He said he would call me later that afternoon if he could get the information he needed, and if not he would be in touch the next day. I still didn't know when I left his office if I had just paid a guy who actually knew what he was doing or if I had just hired a lawyer straight out of Hee Haw.

I left his office, checked out of my motel room near the detention center and headed up Interstate 10 towards the border to find a cheaper motel. Since I was only going to stay as long as it took to find out if Yo could be transferred back to L.A., it didn't make sense to spend any more money on motels than necessary. A cheesy little place near the Sunland Park mall seemed to fill the bill, so I stopped there for the night and crossed my fingers that Durkin would be calling back with some good news by the next day.

THE SCENE OF THE CRIME

Chapter V

Since I had just left Durkin's office, I knew I probably wouldn't get any more news from him until probably the next day at the earliest. So I sat in the motel room for a few minutes trying to decide what to do. I thought that since we had driven all this way to see the white sands at White Sands, that maybe I should go over there anyway and just take some pictures of it. Even though Yolande was now in jail because of our trying to go there, I thought she still might want to see some pictures of what it looked like. Also, someday when this was all behind us, maybe we would be able to look back on it and laugh.

I drove the 50 or 60 odd miles from the motel on the edge of El Paso back to Highway 70, looking out over the vast desert landscape with a different, less innocent attitude. Now I knew there could be enemies in the desert. Enemies that looked like me, talked like me and seemed like friends but were there to cause problems in my life. At least that's how it seemed to me then. I was curious to see if the Border Patrol checkpoint was still there two days later, or if they had pulled up stakes in the middle of the night and moved onward to set a trap for more unsuspecting travelers further down the road.

I got to the point where the road was narrowed down to one lane by the orange traffic cones, and sure enough, the uniformed agent was still standing outside the guard shack building looking for all the world like a National Park ranger collecting entrance fees. But this time, I could see by giving him a closer look that he wasn't wearing a park ranger's uniform. Not that I would have been able to do anything at that point when we first passed through there two days prior. There still was absolutely no way to turn around and go back, nor was there any way to exit before you got to the checkpoint. It was a very well designed, carefully thought out trap.

I rolled to a stop next to the Border Patrol agent. He looked into the car, looked at me and asked, "Are you an American citizen?" Same question, but this time I knew I had the right answer and would be able to slide on through. "Yes", I said. He waved me through. Life is simple if you know the right answers.

I drove about a hundred feet and turned left into the parking lot for White Sands.

I took a look inside the gift shop and asked the woman behind the desk if I had to pay an entrance fee there. No, she said, just drive up the road about a half mile and there would be a booth that you could pay at. I thanked her and looked at some of the knick knacks they had for sale. I wondered if Yolande would think it was funny if I sent her a postcard from White Sands or bought her a little bottle of genuine "real estate", aka sand from the park? Probably not.

I drove into the park, passing bigger and bigger mounds of white, snow-like sand hills the further I drove in. In all honesty, it was actually pretty impressive. Because it was a Monday in January, there were only a few other cars wandering around, so it felt like I had the place pretty much to myself.

I stopped the car a few times, trudged to the top of a large sand dune and tried to take some pictures that would give the viewer some idea of the vast stretches of mile after mile of glistening white dunes. I imagined that this would make the perfect backdrop for a science fiction movie in which space travelers were stuck on a planet with no other form of life as we know it. A place where you could look for miles in any direction and not see another human being. A huge, harsh environment with no trace of pity or compassion for mankind. A place like the one Yolande is in right now, I thought to myself. I took my pictures, drove around a few more sand hills and headed back to El Paso.

Durkin called me late that afternoon. He said he had been to the detention center and had asked to see the official documents that Yolande got admitted on. He said that would tell him whether or not she would be able to have a hearing or not. He told me that he was able to get the name of the guard supervisor who was assigned to her case and left a message to call him back as soon as possible. Beyond that, he said, there wasn't anything anyone could do except wait. I thanked him for his efforts and asked him to call me as soon as he got any new information, and of course he said he would.

I then called the guy I had met a few weeks earlier who was making an independent film I had been cast in. I was going to play a weather man who was the arch rival of the hero, another network TV weather man in Los Angeles. It was a tiny little part with all of two lines in a film that hardly anyone would probably ever see, and I wouldn't even be paid for it. But still, it was a part in a film, and since I had very few film roles under my belt, I was always ready to take a part, any part, in a film. Unfortunately, the first shoot was scheduled for that day.

I had already called and left a message over the weekend saying I wouldn't be able to make the shoot on Monday, and I was so sorry, but I had gone on an out of town trip and my car broke down on Saturday, and I would have to wait until Monday to get it fixed. I promised I would be there as soon as I could, but I knew it wouldn't be before Tuesday at the earliest.

This had actually happened to me and Yolande on a cross country trip the year before, but at that time I didn't have a film shoot to get to the next day, just my regular job. But I figured if it worked once it would work again. Besides I didn't want to get into all the gory details about why she didn't have an up to date visa, etc., etc. I was hoping that by giving them two days' notice that the director would be able to juggle his schedule and move my scene to a different date. I called the number and got ready to leave another message.

To my surprise, someone answered this time, but it wasn't Justin, the director, but a friend of his who was working on the production side of the film. He said yes, Justin had received my voice mail message over the weekend, and not to worry, they had found someone else at the last minute that was able to step in and do my part.

Someone else? I thought. *Who else would be able to say my two lines as perfectly as I could have? Couldn't they just hold off on filming the scene until the weekend?*

I couldn't very well tell him what I was thinking, though, so I just said I was glad they were able to work things out and hung up. So much for another stab at a film acting career.

Oddly enough, I also got a call from a director that had directed a play I had been in about 3 or 4 years earlier called *It Had To Be You* at the Palos Verdes Playhouse. He was directing *Plaza Suite* at the Pacific Palisades theater and wanted to know if I would consider playing a part. I thanked him for his interest, but told him where I was and why I was there and it looked like I wouldn't be able to think about doing any theater or films for quite some time. He was obviously a little stunned, but said he understood the situation and wished me luck in getting everything taken care of quickly. Just my luck, I thought, I get all kinds of offers to do some type of acting work when it's impossible for me to accept them. That seemed to be the story of my life, or at least my acting life.

I got up the next morning, went to a local restaurant for breakfast and then went to the nearest Starbucks to read the paper, drink coffee and hang out until I heard back from Durkin.

It didn't take long. Around 10:45 Durkin called me on my cell and told me he had seen the official document listing out the charges against Yolande and why she had been picked up and placed in the detention center. According to Durkin, it was all cut and dried, just like Red Mustache had told me three days earlier. "She's not going to get any hearing", he said. "They're just going to keep her there until it's time to send her back to Holland." But I told him Margaret Parker had insisted she could get a change of venue and get transferred back to Los Angeles and we could get her status restored there. Well she might know something he didn't know, he told me, but based on what the official record said, and based on the fact that she entered the U.S. on a visa that specifically stated that she could not change her immigration status for *any* reason while she was still in the United States, there was no way she could get a hearing before she got sent back to Holland. I asked him how long that would take and he said he didn't know—three, four weeks at the minimum, maybe longer.

I began to feel more and more hopeless. Durkin told me he would stay in contact with me and give me the name of the deportation officer so I could try to find out when Yolande would be sent back to

Holland, but that was all he could do, all that *anyone* could do as far as he could see. I thanked him again for his efforts and asked him to make sure he called me as soon as he got any information about when Yo would be shipped back to Holland. I was thinking if I could get back to California before that happened, that I could meet with Margaret in Fullerton, explain everything to her and wait for her to come up with some brilliant solution that would fix everything for us. He said he would let me know as soon as he got any more information, but to remember that we were dealing with "the Gestapo" now, and they did things when they were good and ready to do them, and not until then. The more I listened to him, the more he depressed me, so I finally said to call me when he had more news and hung up.

I sat in that Starbucks for a few more minutes thinking about what my answer to the question "Are you both American citizens?" a few days earlier was going to cost me. I didn't care if it cost me every dollar I had. I knew I could get more money eventually. The thing that worried me now more than anything else, was the thought that I might not be able to see Yolande again for a long, long time. *"Maybe never"*, a little voice in the back of my head whispered. "Shut up!" I said to the voice, got into my car and started driving towards California.

EENY, MEENY, MINY, MOE...

Chapter VI

The drive back to California was long and boring. I remember passing by Tucson and remembering there was a ghost town or something like it there that Yo had told me might be interesting to stop and see on our way back from New Mexico. Now the only thing I could think about was getting back to California and meeting with Margaret Parker to try to figure a way out of this god awful mess. I mean all we did was go on a four day mini-vacation! Who would have thought we would have needed a passport or marriage certificate? This was already starting to feel like a bad movie of the week. But the thing that kept me from getting completely depressed was the way Margaret kept sounding like there was a way to fight this. I just had to get back to meet her in Fullerton and find out how.

I stopped overnight in Phoenix and drove on to Long Beach the next day. It was early afternoon when I returned. I parked the car on the street and walked through the doorway into the house that Yo and I had been sharing with Cynthia for the past eleven months.

I could hear voices upstairs as I came through the front door. I knew Cyn had been worried when I talked to her on the phone three days earlier when I called her from New Mexico, and I had sent her a text message telling her I would be back around mid-day on Tuesday, January 31ˢᵗ. I expected her to meet me within a few minutes after I entered the house and grill me about what was going on with Yo. Instead, I heard her talking to someone upstairs, and even though I thought for sure she must have heard me come through the front door, it didn't sound like she was coming down to see who it was. I felt like I had an obligation to talk to her and tell her the latest information I had, even though it really wasn't any more than I had told her when I called her on Saturday. I started up the stairway to her bedroom and upstairs office to give her the latest news.

We went through the predictable question and answer session about what was happening, and how I didn't know any more than I did before, and how I was meeting with Margaret Parker on Friday to get an update on what our options were, etc., etc. She didn't seem all that concerned at the time, which struck me as a little odd in view of how worried she had seemed on the phone three days earlier. But Cyn was a lot like Yo in that respect—she never seemed to worry much about things that seemed to trouble me. Both of them seemed to believe that things would somehow work out for the best.

After I gave her my report, I tried to go back to the business of picking up the pieces and continuing on with my life. But it was actually quite a mess now. I had already lost out on a part in an independent film, which I had hoped would lead to something bigger in a film career, and I also had to cancel out attending some on-line classes for an insurance auditing job which I had planned to begin that week. In addition, I had to learn a presentation I was supposed to give in an interview for a seminar presenter's job I was applying for at the end of the week. But none of that really seemed important now. I just wanted to be able to talk to Yo again as soon as possible, and I hated the fact that I couldn't call her.

She called me on the second or third day. I had been wondering what was taking so long, but typically, Yo didn't see any point in wasting a phone call when there was nothing new to report. I could never make her understand that it helped me just knowing that there wasn't anything new going on, that I really still liked to hear the sound of her voice. I would have been happier if she had been able to tell me something had developed, but even if it hadn't I still wanted to talk to her.

But I also understood why she couldn't call every day also. She had to request money from her locker to buy a phone card and she also had to wait to use the phone. Sometimes that could take a while, considering that she was in a barracks with about sixty other women and there were only three phones for all of them to use. So I tried to get used to the fact that I never knew when she was going to call, and I tried to hang around the house as much as I could in order to be there when she did call. She had to call on the house phone because I usually could not get any kind of decent cell phone reception inside that house.

I kept asking her what she had been told and if anyone had given her any information about how long she would be there. The answer was always no, but she seemed to think that the minimum was somewhere around thirty days. That seemed like an awfully long time to have to sit and cool your heels all day, and I was determined to find a way to get her out of there sooner than that. Of course, she took it all in stride, but I wanted her out of there as soon as possible so we could get on with our lives.

I went to see Margaret Parker seven days after Yo had been picked up in New Mexico. Margaret listened to the whole story calmly and patiently, and to her credit, never tried to make feel guilty about leaving the state with Yolande, the way Catherine Smith had done when I called her.

Margaret asked me about my experience with Durkin and I told her I thought he was a good old boy, but he hadn't really given me much hope. Margaret said she was a little disappointed in how long it took to get a return call from him, which was something I had been annoyed with too. She felt that he should have tried to change the venue to L.A. and have Yolande go before a judge there who knew immigration law better than any Border Patrol agents. She wanted me to find out from Durkin who the supervisor was in El Paso that she would have to talk to and I told her I knew he was trying to do that, but he still hadn't been able to get that information from what he had told me. She said we could fill out the request for a waiver of penalty there and have it ready to submit once Yo got returned to L.A.

We talked about all the shit that people have to go through just to be able to be in the United States if they're not natural born citizens. She told me a horror story about a classmate of her son's who had been born in the U.S., but because his mother had never become legal, she was getting deported and the son was going to be deported with her. She told me she would get started on filling out the forms and set a date for me to come back to sign them.

For the next week or so, Yo would call me every three or four days, telling me about her new "prison life." She lived in a barracks with about fifty or sixty other women, most of them Latinas from Mexico, Guatemala or Central or South America. Unlike her, most of them were very worried about being deported back to their home country. Some of them spoke English, but many of them didn't. The ones who did told her some depressing stories.

One of the women was seeking political asylum from some country in Asia, and she faced severe harm, as in death and/or torture if she got sent back because she had "opposed the government" that was now in power. Actually the only thing she had done was to lend a raincoat to her cousin who had been identified as a terrorist against Burma as a result of his involvement in protests against the Burmese government's anti-Christian policies. This meant she had given aid to a "terrorist" so she too was then classified as a terrorist by Burma and the United States!

Because she was an illegal immigrant, she couldn't stay in the U.S., but her lawyers had successfully filed motions to keep her from returning to her home country because of the danger she would face upon her return. The problem was she couldn't stay in the U.S. and they couldn't send her back to where she had come from, so she had to try to petition a third country to allow her to go there. All of this had taken nearly two years! She had been sitting in prison in El Paso for nearly two years because our government would not make an exception and grant her political asylum because she had committed the heinous crime of trying to live peaceably in the U.S.

There were several other women who had told Yo similar horror stories which caused them to be detained for up to a year or longer, depending on the circumstances of their arrest.

As she told me all this, I began to worry about how long it would take before she could get out of there. Maybe thirty days wasn't such a long time after all.

DETENTION CENTER COMEDY CLUB

Chapter VII

Yo later told me about some of the silliness of her prison life. The guards there would go to great lengths to make sure the male prisoners and female prisoners never crossed paths. Whenever a male prisoner had to walk through the grounds outside, the female prisoners would be kept physically separated by the guards until he passed by. She told me how ridiculous it seemed for all the women to have to be held back a minimum of ten feet whenever they had to be taken out of the barracks for various reasons and they had to pass by one of the male detainees. The guards even had walkie talkies to let each other know that a female was approaching, what doorway she was going through, what room she was going into, etc., etc., even though all the men were accompanied by armed guards! Yo said they made the women feel like they were walking time bombs, having to be monitored through every step of their journey.

There were other aspects of prison life that Yo found funny also. There was the ICE agent who seemed to like standing in the barracks when the women passed by with one leg propped up on a chair and his sunglasses on. Yo thought he was trying to look exceptionally cool, and he had the "ICE" emblem on his cap, which stood for "Immigration Control and Enforcement." This all led Yo to believe that he thought he was cooler than your average rap singer, and since he was wearing an ICE emblem, she decided he was trying to act like Vanilla Ice, the former rap star. When the women were walking two by two through the barracks, as they were told they had to do, he would stand with one leg propped on the chair, watching them through his sunglasses. So when Yo passed by, she couldn't resist whispering "Ice, Ice, baby!" to the other girls in line, as an allusion to one of the lines from

Vanilla Ice's song. The other women told her to be careful, that she would get in trouble for saying things like that, but she couldn't help herself.

Yo also mentioned that for some strange reason, there seemed to be a definite trend toward hiring obese men and women to be detention center guards. She noticed that approximately ten percent of the guards seemed to be "normal sized", while the remainder seemed to range from the noticeably overweight to the extremely overweight. There was always one guard stationed inside the barracks, round the clock, whose only job was to sit behind a desk and watch the women detainees, who in turn watched the guards, who watched the detainees, etc., etc. It probably shouldn't be too surprising that the job attracted the more sedentary elements of the population. However, Yo was very impressed that one of the women guards who sat behind a desk for 8 hours a day watching the detainees and trying to find something else to do, was so obese that she needed two chairs to sit on!

Meal times were particularly amusing. Approximately 150 women would be marched into the dining room, two by two. Once they arrived at a certain point they would be stopped to wait for one of the guards, who took it upon himself to act as the maitre'd for the detention center to call out the number of women who could proceed to be seated. He would do so by calling out loudly, "I've got one, two three, four, FIVE LADIES," and then motioning them to go forward. If they only had space for four it would be "FOUR LADIES," if they needed six, it was "SIX LADIES," and so on. The women would then pick up a tray and go through a cafeteria style line to get their food.

During the mealtime there would be anywhere from 8 to 10 guards walking through the dining room. They would often tell the detainees "no talking" if anyone dared to whisper or giggle amongst themselves while they were eating. They would allow each detainee no more than 15 or 20 minutes to eat their meal because immediately after the women, approximately 600 male detainees would have to be fed. However, why so many guards were needed for this duty was a mystery, considering that the most dangerous thing the women had in their possession while they were eating was their plastic "sporks"—a spoon and fork combination—which would not appear to be very useful in the event of a riot!

Getting the right sized shoes was another adventure. She started out getting shoes which were too big. She asked for a size 5, but they gave her a pair of a man's size 5, which was the equivalent of a woman's size 8. When she told the guard her shoes were too big, she was told that, in order to get a different pair of shoes issued, she would need a *prescription* from the center's doctor for her own "safety and welfare"!

She eventually got the prescription needed to get smaller shoes, but it took a week and a half to do it—and then they were still too big. (The guards said they didn't have any women's size 5 shoes, but there were many women in the facility with smaller feet than Yo.)

Twice a week, the detainees were given their barracks clothes. One guard with three helpers would come into the barracks with containers of laundry. The women would then stand in line and wait for the helpers to hand out their clothes onto a table.

During one of these sessions, Yo got to the front of the line and was given an extra large pair of pants and top. All of the women prisoners were given larger sizes to wear than they needed because the guards did not want to take a chance that the women might excite some of the male prisoners when they occasionally had to be taken outside of the barracks and pass by them. However, Yo had been wearing extra large pants for the previous week, which were so large for her that they chafed. Naturally, when it got to be her turn to get new clothes, she asked the helper to give her a large instead of an extra large pair.

The guard in charge of issuing the barracks clothes immediately snapped at her "'Extra Large!" When Yo told her the extra large pants were chafing her, the guard responded with "You wear what I give you!" She of course offered no explanation as to why she insisted that Yo wear pants that were incredibly large for her, and momentarily walked away to scrutinize something else.

While she was distracted, Yo quietly asked the woman who was handing out the clothes for a large size pants, and the helper obliged by disobeying the guard and giving her a large instead of an extra large. Yo thanked her and left the table to change into her newly issued prize so she could stop the chafing caused by the extra large pants.

About an hour and a half later, while she was eating one of her meals in the dining room, the same guard who told Yo she had to wear the extra large pants noticed that she was wearing a smaller size. She immediately confronted her and asked her why she wasn't wearing the extra large pants she had told her to wear. Yo told her again that the extra large pants caused her legs to chafe when she wore them. The guard then left the dining room and returned a few minutes later with another pair of extra large pants. She told Yo to change into the larger pants. Yo told her "No!"

At this point the guard became flustered and went to tell the ICE officer who was on duty in the dining room at the time that Yo was causing problems and needed some type of disciplinary action. Yo waited until the guard left the room and walked over to tell the ICE officer her side of the story. He listened to her explanation and seemed to be understanding about her predicament. However, just as she had to do to be able to get smaller shoes to wear, the ICE officer told her she would now need a prescription from the detention center's doctor to justify her need to wear a smaller size pants! And of course, this had to be arranged with the *morning* guard who would be on duty the next day!

Yo waited patently to explain her situation to the morning guard the next day and eventually was allowed to see the doctor to get her prescription for *smaller pants* filled! Needless to say, that was the only time she ever had to see a doctor to ask for a prescription for smaller sized clothing!

One thing the guards seemed to have in common was that they would never admit if they made a mistake. They also seemed to enjoy treating the women in the barracks as prisoners rather than detainees, and went out of their way to find subtle ways to antagonize them. For example, although the women in the barracks were under strict orders to be silent and go to sleep as quickly as possible after lights out each night, the guards made no effort to keep quiet to allow them to sleep while they made their nocturnal rounds. They would routinely walk through the barracks at night with keys jangling from their belts and walkie-talkies squawking loudly as they passed by the beds of the women attempting to sleep. They would also shine flashlights directly on the women's faces to make sure they were in their beds and attempting to sleep. On top of that, they would often talk, joke and laugh with each other as loudly as they would during the middle of the day, giving no thought at all to the noise they were creating while the detainees were trying to get some rest.

Two of the guards who were particularly disliked by the detainees were nicknamed "De Groote" (The Big) and "De Kleine" (The Small) by Yo. "De Groote" was a tall woman who barked out orders like a drill sergeant. She was also known as "The Green Book" by some of the detainees because of her penchant for reading the detention center rules from the official green rule book. "De Kleine" was a smaller woman who liked to yell out "Silencio" to the detainees any time she heard anyone talking or making any noise whatsoever.

During her time at El Paso, Yo kept notes on the bizarre goings on. She typically wrote her notes in Dutch which was a good way to keep them private. However, since there was nowhere else to store them, she would leave them stacked in a pile underneath her mattress.

One day while Yo was in the library, De Groote found her notes under the bed. She had to know whose they were since they were not written in English or Spanish, and Yo was the only detainee who would write anything in Dutch. Yet, for some reason she decided that she should throw Yo's notes in the trash. When Yo returned from the library, she noticed her notes were missing and she asked De Groote about them. The guard told her she didn't know whose notes they were, and that she asked several people if they belonged to them but they all told her "no," so she decided to throw them out!

Yo was understandably upset, but there was really nothing she could do about it besides seethe. The only satisfaction she received was seeing De Groote get chewed out by her supervisor who read about the incident in the guard's log that afternoon. Apparently De Groote was too dumb to know she had invaded a detainee's privacy or so arrogant that she thought she could record it in the official record without any fear of reprimand. In this case, at least, she turned out to be wrong.

Intentionally or unintentionally, many of the guards treated the detainees condescendingly and often antagonized them for no apparent reason. One example of this occurred when the woman who was a political refugee from Asia had to go to a hospital outside the detention center for a routine check up.

She had high blood pressure and another medical condition that required her to go to a specialist outside the compound on a monthly basis. Normally this required her to get on a bus inside the detention center and make her monthly visit to the doctor's office in El Paso, accompanied by a guard.

During one of her visits, she was assigned to a new male guard who for some reason felt that he had to make sure the Asian woman knew who was the prisoner and who was the guard. He insisted that the 48 year old Asian woman was a threat to go anywhere outside the detention center, even with an armed guard by her side, and insisted that she be hand cuffed and ankle cuffed before leaving the detention center grounds.

When he told San Wa (not her real name) that she had to wear hand cuffs and leg cuffs before going to her doctor appointment, she decided that she had been pushed as far as she could go and she refused to do it. The guard put on a temporary show of authority and demanded that San Wa comply with his orders. However, to her credit, she again refused.

This was very embarrassing to the new guard and could have easily led to a relatively dangerous incident had it not been for the intercession of some of the other guards who happened to be in the reception area at the time. Apparently even they felt this was going a bit too far and managed to ridicule the new guard to the point where he ultimately swallowed his pride and decided that letting San Wa go to her doctor's appointment uncuffed could be done without imposing any significant danger to the citizens of El Paso.

In another instance, a Muslim woman from North Africa was harassed because of her attempt to worship according to the custom of her faith. Although the center allowed a Catholic priest to visit the detainees every two weeks to hand out rosaries, religious pamphlets and mass schedules, there was no such accommodation provided for any other religion. In order to be allowed to wear long sleeves in place of the short sleeves provided from her detention center uniform and the headscarf which Muslim women wear for their prayer rituals, she had asked the Catholic priest to submit a signed note to the administration asking that this be allowed. The priest had indicated that he would do so and she considered the matter closed.

However, during one of her five daily prayer sessions, one of the new guards at the center told her she was in violation of the clothing requirements and demanded that she wear a short sleeve shirt like everyone else and lose the headscarf. The woman was deeply religious and felt that she had a duty to follow her Muslim teachings regarding her clothing. She explained this to the guard and also told her that the priest had provided a note to the administration allowing these exceptions, but to no avail. The guard demanded that she remove her headscarf and switch to short sleeves by the next day or the guard would file a formal reprimand.

This caused the African woman an enormous amount of stress and she started crying openly, asking the other women what she should do. Yo and the other detainees tried to calm her down, telling her to ask the guards if she could call a nearby convent to try to locate the priest who had provided the note and ask him to intercede. The guard who came on duty after the first guard who started all the fuss told her that she would check to find out if there was indeed a note in her file from the priest who said he would request her clothing exceptions to be approved.

But after that nothing happened. Yo said that the guards were constantly being rotated among different barracks and different stations, so that the guard who initially told the African woman she could not wear her headscarf either forgot about the issue or decided it wasn't worth pursuing it further. It apparently wasn't all that important after all, but it allowed the guard to put pressure on a detainee and somehow make her feel superior because she could inflict needless stress on another human being.

The detainees who worked in the kitchen were the internal "grapevine" for the barracks. They would often tell them about some of the incompetence they witnessed from working directly with the guards. They told the women about an escape attempt that occurred while Yo was there.

Apparently, one of the male detainees who was allowed to work in the "depot," or main reception area, had found a way to steal some street clothes from a locker. He even got outside the building and climbed over one of the barbed wire fences that surrounded the center. However, in doing so he was badly cut by the barbed wire and was spotted walking down the road outside the center by a private citizen.

The citizen noticed how badly the man was bleeding and placed a 911 call for an ambulance to take him to a hospital for treatment. However, before the ambulance could arrive, the man was captured by the guards and returned to the detention center.

Shortly afterwards, the private ambulance arrived and the paramedics went into the detention center to find the man who needed treatment. However, the receptionist and guards on duty told the paramedics they must have been misinformed and refused to admit that anyone had been injured while trying to escape. The outside world could not find out that someone had nearly escaped the El Paso detention center!

No matter what happened in the detention center, however, Yo always seemed to find the humor in almost any situation. She even went so far as to gently taunt the guards whenever the opportunity arose to let them know they couldn't break her spirit.

Periodically an officer from ICE would visit the barracks to check up on the guards and make sure everything was under control. The visitors from ICE could be either male or female. However, whenever a male visitor was due the women detainees were told that they had to stay away from the showers and the bathroom until told otherwise because the guards watching the closed circuit camera "could see everything there." Even if they were already in the showers and soaped up, they were told to get out immediately and put their clothes on. Within ten minutes the male ICE officer would appear in the barracks.

Most of the women there were very modest and concerned about anyone seeing them without any clothes, even by the other women in the barracks. In fact, most of the women detainees would take showers *with their underwear on*, whether any male officers were expected or not, and then take them off later when they could cover themselves while toweling off.

Yo, of course, had no such inhibitions. In fact, once she found out that there was a closed circuit camera in the ceiling watching their every move, she decided to liven up the show for whoever was watching the monitor that day. She decided to forego any pretense of modesty and stepped out from behind the shower wall after taking her shower and didn't bother to go through the ritual of covering herself with a towel. Instead, she simply walked out of the shower area completely naked, waved at the closed circuit camera in the ceiling and yelled out *"Yoo hoo, boys!"*

Some of the other detainees were a little shocked at Yo's lack of inhibitions, but that was something she didn't worry about. Yo didn't worry about a lot of things that other people did. Even being stuck in a detention center in El Paso didn't even phase her most of the time.

Throughout this period, I would get calls from Durkin every three or four days, telling me he was trying to set up a meeting with the "deportation officer" at the detention center to find out if Yo could get her venue changed. He said that he had to see the formal charges they planned on filing against her to determine if he could file a motion. After about a week of trying to arrange a meeting he called me while I was at Venice Beach with my daughter, who was visiting from Wisconsin.

"I finally got a hold of him today," he said with his thick Texas accent. "They ain't gonna' give her a hearing. They're just gonna' send her back."

When I asked him why they could do this, he said it was because of the visa she had signed. Apparently, old Red Mustache in New Mexico was right—at least according to Durkin. Because she had signed a visa that specifically stated that she could not change her immigration status for any reason while she was still in the U.S., she would have to go back to Holland and we would have to try to petition to get her back from there.

I thanked Durkin for his efforts and told him I would try to follow up with Margaret Parker and do whatever else needed to be done from California. Besides, he already told me there was noting else he could do, so I was hoping Margaret could come up with something he didn't know about.

When I told Margaret about this latest development a few days later, she still insisted that we could get Yo's venue changed. All we had to do was enter a "stay" on her deportation order so that Margaret could issue a request to change the venue of her detainment, and she felt confident that she could have a judge in L.A. County order a hearing on the matter and release her until the hearing took place. When I asked her how long this whole process would take she said, "Well, it'll take a day to issue the stay on her deportation order, then it could take two to three weeks for them to send her to L.A. Then we can get her released, but depending on how bad the courts are backed up, it could take a year to a year and a half to get it all resolved."

When I told this to Yo on the phone the next day, I thought she would be excited to hear that we could stop her deportation order and that she could be back in California, out of jail within a couple of weeks, if not sooner. Surprisingly, the first thing she said was, "So, in the meantime, I am stuck in the U.S. and can't go anywhere else, right?" I told her that was my understanding and asked her why that would be a problem. She said "Because right now, I am pretty much fed up with the United States. It has been over five years since I saw my family in Holland, and if I cannot leave the U.S. for a year and a half or longer then I say, let them send me back!"

I was a bit surprised to hear her say this, because it was the first time she hadn't sounded her usual upbeat self. But I could understand why she was getting fed up. It had been almost three weeks already that she had been stuck in a prison in El Paso for the heinous crime of trying to go to a National Park with me, and even though it seemed to me that she and her family were not extremely close, I could understand that she would want to see her parents again before another year to a year and a half had passed. Besides, that was just the time frame it might take to have the hearing that would allow her to apply for a new visa. After that it might take another 6 months before she got her temporary visa and another 6 months to a year after that before she got the famous green card.

Given the fact that it could be another two to three years before she could return to see her family in Holland, I could totally sympathize with her. There was one other option that Margaret had mentioned the last time I talked to her, however. She had told me that after the visa application and waiver of penalty forms had been prepared, it might possibly be quicker for me to go to Holland and file the forms with Yolande at the U.S. embassy in Amsterdam. Margaret thought that this could possibly be done in a much shorter time frame. The only catch was, once she left, Yolande could not *return* to the U.S. until the temporary visa was provided to her. Still, if it meant waiting in the U.S. and not being able to leave for another two years or going to Holland and submitting the paperwork there and not being able to return to the U.S. for 6 months to a year, Yo was adamant that she would only do the latter. She had had all she could stand with the ridiculously excessive immigration laws in the U.S. and did not want to stay here any longer than she had to.

Under the circumstances, I completely understood how she felt. I was just surprised that the anger and bitterness were finally coming out. The fact that she was finally showing the effects of being in the detention center for so long with almost nothing to do made me realize that I had to choose the shortest option, whatever it was.

The next day I called Margaret Parker and told her to forget putting through a "stop" on Yo's deportation order. She didn't want to do that if it meant she could not leave the U.S. for up to two years or longer. Instead we had decided that it would be better for me to go with her to the U.S. embassy in Holland and plead with them for mercy.

Margaret was a little disappointed that she wasn't going to be able to make them change the venue and have Yo sent back to California the way she kept insisting they should have done in the first place, but she also understood where Yo was coming from. She told me she would have all the forms prepared and ready for me to take with me when I left.

It looked like I was going to Holland.

LET'S GO TO HOLLAND!

Chapter VIII

The trick about making plans to go to Holland was that I didn't know when Yo was going to be sent back, and nobody at the detainee center would tell us. As I later found out, we weren't even supposed to know. Yo was given a number for the Dutch consulate in Texas, but they told her they could not do anything to speed the process along, nor could they give her any information about how long it might take. However, a contact who knew someone at the Dutch consulate was somehow able to find out and eventually passed the date on to me. (Call me paranoid, but I still don't want to reveal any names in case it would get someone in trouble for trying to be human to us.) Once I did find out, I was a little amazed at the date. Yo was scheduled to be sent back on March 17th—over six weeks after the date she was picked up at White Sands! I was wondering how to break the news to her when she called me.

As usual, I didn't have to worry about Yo. She had found out about the return date from her Dutch consulate contact too, and it didn't surprise her in the least. She had talked to enough women who had been there 30 days or longer to know that it wasn't going to be a quick turn around. Even though, the only thing that had to be done, from my viewpoint, was to set up a date with the Dutch consulate to have her returned to Holland and make arrangements with an airline to send her back, there was enough paperwork involved and enough detainees waiting to get kicked out of the U.S. that it normally took a minimum of 3 or 4 months. Even so, Yo did not seem depressed on upset in the slightest way. If anyone was angry or upset about the whole situation, it was me. But then again, it was mostly my fault that she was in this mess to begin with.

Once we knew the actual date, I started making arrangements to meet her in Holland. I found out that she would be flown from El Paso to Atlanta, and then catch a flight from there to Amsterdam.

The only problem with that was my flight to Amsterdam from L.A. was scheduled to arrive a half hour before her flight. Since I had never traveled outside of the U.S. on my own before, and did not speak any other language besides English, I was a little nervous about arriving in a country by myself where I didn't speak the language and didn't know anybody. But we didn't really have any choice, so I went ahead and booked the flight.

After the flight had been booked, I decided it was time to meet the folks. I got Yo's parents' phone number from the erasable message board on Cyn's refrigerator and dialed it. When her mom answered, I hoped she could understand English well enough for me to get the message across. I started out by saying "Hello, this is Mike, Yolande's husband from America."

It felt a little weird to be introducing myself on the phone like that, but what else could I say? To my surprise, her mom sounded like she understood perfectly and was able to speak English very well. I told her that Yo was going to be sent back to Holland on March 17th and she told me she was very glad that I called, and that she had been very worried about her. After a few minutes, she handed the phone over to someone else. A woman's voice came on the line and she told me she was Yolande's sister-in-law, Dees, who just happened to be at Yo's parents' house as part of a birthday party. She spoke very good English and I told her everything I knew about when Yo would be returning and life inside the detention center at El Paso.

She also said she was glad I called and said Yo's mom was very relieved to hear that she was safe and sound and would be back in Holland soon. I also told them I would be joining Yo in Amsterdam so we could go to the U.S. embassy and get the ball rolling to get her visa reinstated. Dees told me everyone there was glad to get the news, and then said goodbye. I hung up and started thinking about what I had to do next.

I began to phase out my pet sitting and dog walking business appointments. There hadn't been that many to begin with, since I had just started the business about 4 months earlier, but I did have some appointments for the next few weeks that had to be re-scheduled. The weeks started dragging by, partly because I never knew when Yo would be calling, so I tried to stick around the house for most mornings just in case she called. When she did call every three or four days, there was never any real news to report, but it was pretty interesting to hear her describe some of the details about her daily "prison life."

Yo told me that the worst thing about being in "the clink" was the boredom she had to deal with each day. The detention center guards would wake her and the other 50 or 60 women she shared the barracks with around 6:00 a.m. each morning to have breakfast at 6:30 a.m. and then spend all but one hour of the rest of the day sitting around with nothing to do. There was one television set which was usually tuned to the station that the lone guard stationed inside the barracks wanted to watch, which usually featured some kind of violent, adventure type B movie or a Spanish TV program. The women generally sat around chatting or sleeping since there wasn't much of anything else to do. There were a few books and magazines available, but most of them were in Spanish and most of them had already been read by most of the detainees there. The few books written in English were prized possessions because Yo and a few of the other women were not fluent in Spanish. After she told me this, I started to try to send a few books to here every couple of weeks. I couldn't send too many at a time because the guards seemed to dislike getting large packages, but they would allow smaller packages with only 3 or 4 books or magazines inside. The other women who could read English were always very happy when Yo's "CARE package" arrived because it gave them something to read for a week or so. Yo decided she would just leave the books once she got shipped out, so we basically started an English book library for the other women in the barracks there.

One of the other discoveries Yo made was that, although there was a weight machine in the "exercise yard" (which was really not much more than an asphalt parking lot), most of the other women had no idea how to use it, so Yo started an informal training class to show them what to do with it. This eventually progressed to the point where she organized a few informal exercise classes to give the women something else to do besides sit, talk and sleep all day.

None of this really seemed to bother her much, or if it did, she always kept it pretty much to herself. After I booked my flight to Amsterdam, I set up one more visit with Margaret Parker to make sure we had all the forms filled out that I needed to take to the U.S. embassy when I got to Amsterdam. Yo was able to write to her parents and let them know when we would be arriving, and since it would be on a Saturday, we planned on staying in Amsterdam until Monday when we could go to the embassy and file the application forms. The Dutch consulate contact had told us the process would take a minimum of 10 to 12 weeks, so we planned on staying with Yo's parents and seeing the sites in Holland until then.

Life continued to creep along until the big day. I had talked to Yo on the phone to find out what clothes she wanted me to bring and anything else she needed and I packed what I thought I would need in Holland. Everything was packed and ready to go the night before I left. I made arrangements with Cyn to leave my car in the parking lot at her restaurant so no one had to move it once a week for the street sweeper. She also volunteered to drop me off at the airport, so all I needed was to get a phone call from Yo confirming that her flight was still on for the 17th and no last minute changes had been made.

I waited to hear from Yo that Friday and made sure I stayed around the house as much as possible. I really wanted to get a call from her saying that she had finally been notified that she would be leaving on the 17th so that I could feel sure that I would be able to find her once I got to Amsterdam. No such luck. The day went by without any phone call from Yo and then the night went by the same way. I was beginning to wonder if I knew what I was doing by flying to a country that I had never been to before, didn't speak the language, didn't know anyone there and wasn't really sure that I knew when Yo would be arriving and on what flight.

I waited until about 10:00 p.m. and then I knew Yo would not be calling, since their lights out time was 10:00 p.m. in El Paso, which was an hour ahead of me. I was going to have to go to Holland on my own, have faith that she would be arriving on the next flight behind me, and that we would go to the embassy two days later and get the whole thing resolved. I also knew that even though I might be worried about all of the hundreds of things I could imagine might go wrong, that Yo would not be concerned in the least. In her mind, everything always worked out for the best. I tried to make myself believe that too and tried to go to sleep so I could get up at 6:00 a.m. to have Cyn drive me to the airport in time for my flight. I tried to mentally keep my fingers crossed and hoped that things would go right for a change.

UNDER AMSTERDAM SKIES

Chapter IX

I woke up around 4:30, got dressed and waited for Cyn to come downstairs around 6:00 for the trip to the airport. She dropped me off at the terminal and wished me all the luck in the world in getting Yo back to America. I got on a plane that morning and the next day I landed in Amsterdam. The whole trip was extremely uneventful, one might even say boring. The only excitement occurred during my layover in New York.

Since I would be connecting to Amsterdam through John F. Kennedy airport in New York, I assumed there would be plenty of St. Patrick's Day decorations and green beer in the pubs to celebrate the holiday. To my surprise, not one of airport pubs had any decorations at all, and the one I stopped in didn't even have any green beer! Having grown up on the south side of Chicago, not having a glass of green beer on St. Patrick's Day seemed almost un-American. However, since I really had no alternative I had to settle for two glasses of regular beer and a silent toast to St. Patrick.

The main reason I stopped at the airport pub, however, was because I had about a three hour layover and didn't know what else to do. I had gone to the counter for my gate at 4:00 p.m., but it was empty. Since my flight didn't leave until a few minutes after 6:00, I figured I would come back in an hour or so. I made a couple of phone calls from the pub, so I got back to the gate counter a little later than I planned, about 5:40 p.m.

When I presented my boarding pass to the girl at the counter, she looked at me and said "I'm sorry. This flight is all sold out. You'll have to fly stand-by."

I couldn't believe what I was hearing. I had to be on this flight or else Yolande would be landing in Amsterdam tomorrow morning and wouldn't find me waiting for her like we planned. On top of that, she didn't have a cell phone, so there was no way I could contact her to let her know if and when I would be coming on a later flight.

"How can it be sold out?" I asked the ticket agent. "I've got my boarding pass right here!"

"I'm sorry, Sir, but I called for all ticketed passengers ten minutes ago and you didn't come up to the counter, so we sold off your seat to a stand-by passenger."

"You can't do that!" I told her. "I've got to get on that plane to meet my wife in Amsterdam tomorrow!"

"I'm sorry, Sir," she said, looking at my ticket. "There's nothing else I can do, you should have checked in at the gate as soon as you got here from L.A."

"I did, but there was nobody here at four o'clock," I said.

"Oh, no, sir, I've been here since quarter to four."

"You lying sack of shit," I thought to myself, but I decided it wouldn't do me much good to start screaming at this point. But I would if it looked like I was going to miss that flight.

I asked her what we could do, and she said she would make an announcement offering cash and a hotel room for the night to anyone who voluntarily gave up their seat for another flight out tomorrow. Since I had purchased a ticket in advance and was merely "late" to the gate, I would get the first crack at any tickets that were given up. Well, actually the second crack, because there was another woman there in the same boat as me, but she wasn't complaining about nobody being at the counter when she arrived, so I assumed she really was late. Anyhow, two passengers decided they couldn't pass up the $400 per ticket offer, so they decided to take the cash, hotel room and a later flight and sold their tickets back to the airline. The lady in front of me and I both got to get on our flight after all, but it was pretty tense up until then. Luckily that was the only problem I had getting to Amsterdam.

Sometime during the 8 or 9 hour flight from New York I managed to get almost an hour's worth of sleep. I never sleep well on a plane and sometimes I can't get to sleep at all because I can never stretch my legs as far as I need to in order to get comfortable. (I've always been too poor or too cheap to fly First Class.) This time I must have finally gotten tired enough to lose consciousness for an hour or so, and when I woke up I heard the pilot announce that we had started our descent into Schiopol Airport in Amsterdam.

The plane landed without any problem whatsoever and I walked out into the terminal of a very clean, modern airport. I looked around for the familiar "arrival/departure" screens that we have in almost all American airports, but I couldn't find any. I checked the information I had from the Dutch consulate about the flight number that Yo was supposed to arrive on, and which gate, etc., and I realized that her arrival gate was supposedly the one right next to mine!

I sat down on a chair in the waiting area. While I was waiting, I checked my watch and wondered if Yo's flight was still on schedule. I thought I might call the Dutch consulate contact that had provided the information to us, but I then realized that my cell phone did not work outside the U.S. On top of that I couldn't even open the contact screen that listed the phone number for Yo's parents. "Great job, Michael," I said to myself. "You're now in a country where you don't speak the official language, you don't know anyone here and you can't contact anyone you even *kind of* know. In addition you're waiting at an airport for a plane that you don't know for sure when it will land, and you're *hoping* that your wife will walk out of it once it does—however, if she ***doesn't***, you have no way of contacting her to find out if she is still on her way, and if so, when and where you might be able to meet her. ***Excellent planning, old boy!***"

I decided to ask one of the airline agents working at the gate counter if they knew if the next flight arriving at the gate was the flight from Atlanta. She didn't know. I asked her if it was the flight number Yolande was supposed to arrive on. She didn't know that either. I wasn't making a whole lot of progress in trying to figure out what to do next, so I did the only thing left—I sat there and waited.

After one of the longest half hours of my life, I saw a plane slowly descending out of the clouds, landing on the runway and taxiing towards the gate. I waited for the plane to roll up to the gate and open its doors. People started walking out. First a group of ten, then another group of ten or fifteen, then another twenty, then another ten, etc., etc. I stood there, waiting for Yo and thinking she was probably sitting in the last seat of the last row, and every other person on the plane would be getting off before her—*if* she got off at all.

After what seemed like about two hundred people had walked out of the plane, Yo finally appeared, laughing and joking with the airline stewards who were walking alongside her. I finally let out a big sigh of relief and waited for her to turn in her paperwork to one of the airline ticket agents. She walked up to me with a big, relaxed smile on her face like she was just returning from a week's vacation. I kissed her and said "Ich hou van yau!" Then I said "What the hell took you so long? Were you really the last one on the plane?"

As usual, she just laughed.

NEXT STOP:
UDEN

Chapter X

Yo told me that she had to have two guards (one male, one female) escort her on the flight from El Paso to Atlanta. They all had lunch together at the El Paso airport, and they both tried to be as pleasant as possible under the circumstances. Then, they flew with her to Atlanta and stayed with her until they transferred her passport and other paperwork to the stewardess on her flight. According to what they told Yo, they then had to stay at the airport in Atlanta and watch her plane physically take off before they could turn around and fly back to El Paso!

Once she arrived in Amsterdam, the stewardess gave her passport and paperwork to two Dutch immigration officers. They asked her why she had been deported from the United States. She told them that it was strictly because she had overstayed her visa. They both looked at each other and shook their heads. Apparently they thought it had to be for something far more serious.

After hearing her story, I understood why Yo actually *was* the last person to get off the plane!

We went down to the baggage claim area to pick up my suitcases. I was excited to be in Holland and surprised at how most of the signs in the airport were in English as well as Dutch. Most of all, I was happy to be back together with Yo after nearly 7 weeks of separation. She was still her same old self, acting like she had just endured nothing more inconvenient than a longer lay over than usual at her last stop. After the usual wait, we got my bags off the carousel, checked out through the customs exit and walked out into the streets of Amsterdam.

The first thing I noticed when we got out the door was that it was COLD in Holland! Living in California the last 16 years had made me forget what winter (or in this case, early spring) was like in other parts of the world. The other thing I realized pretty quickly was that my suitcases were pretty damn heavy when you had to carry them for any distance. I had made a point of trying to pack up as much as I thought I would need for 12 weeks, but I hadn't stopped to think about how hard it might be to carry them around, especially in a place where the temperature was still in the forties. And, since we were in Amsterdam and I had absolutely no idea as to where to go, I simply had to follow Yo's lead.

First we had to get on the train that connected Schiopol Airport to Amsterdam, about 10 miles away. We had planned to stay in Amsterdam until the U.S. embassy opened on Monday so that we could go and file the forms to re-instate Yo's visa as soon as possible. So the first order of business was to find a hotel to check into for three days. However, since it became obvious that walking anywhere with the two overstuffed suitcases was going to be awkward, to say the least, we decided to store them in a locker at the central train station and then go searching for a hotel.

Although it was still pretty cold outside, I was glad to be wandering the streets with Yo, looking at all the old buildings, the canals, and experiencing the crowds walking everywhere in the city. After stopping in a few of the hotels on the main street, we came to the realization that most of the hotels in the city were already sold out for the weekend. Why? Because it was St. Patrick's Day and the city was swamped with out of towners, mostly Brits, who wanted to celebrate the weekend in Amsterdam! I told Yo that I was surprised so many foreigners would come to Amsterdam to celebrate St. Patrick's Day. She said, "Well, we've got booze, hookers and drugs here, so what else would anyone want?" Good old Yo, always looking at life from a practical point of view!

Since it looked like we weren't going to have much luck finding a place to stay in the city that weekend, Yo decided that it would make more sense to stay with her parents in Uden for two nights and come back to go to the U.S. embassy on Monday. We found ourselves a phone outside the visitor's center near the train station and Yo called her parents.

After about an hour on the train, we arrived at the station in Oss. We picked up our bags, got off the train and before I could even see anyone waiting for us, Yo said "There she is!" and started walking quickly towards the end of the train platform.

Although I had talked to her on the phone twice, I had never even seen a picture of Yo's mother until now. Based on what Yo had told me about her, I half expected to see a woman who was so practical that she might not even bother with the formality of saying hello, but would just herd us over to her car and tell us to get in. Instead, I was greeted by a woman who seemed to be in her sixties, about Yo's height with short, closely cropped grey hair and a vague resemblance to her. But the most surprising thing about her was her laughter.

She started laughing as soon as she saw Yo. When they got close enough, they gave each other hugs and the obligatory three Dutch kisses (right cheek, left cheek and then right cheek again). Then Yo introduced me to her mom and, of course the first thing she did was laugh. It was not the first time I would be wondering what it was Rieke Wassenberg was laughing about, but I soon learned not to think too much about it. Many people have told me over the years that I look too hard for answers to questions that no one else even thinks about, so I decided not to try to understand Rieke's sense of humor. Besides, since I didn't speak Dutch except for a few phrases, I probably wouldn't understand her reasoning anyway. The important thing was she and Yo's father, Piet, were letting us stay at their home for free while we tried to get the paperwork filed by the U.S. embassy. What else did I need to know?

Yo decided I should sit in the front passenger seat to have the seat with the most leg room, and she would sit in the back while her mom drove. Thus began the half hour trip to Uden, where Yo grew up and her parents still lived. During this time, I found myself looking out the window at the relatively flat, pastoral landscape, interrupted every few miles by the apartments and houses of the various small towns along the route. Yo and her mother seemed to have quite a bit to say to each other and since it was almost all in Dutch, I understood none of it, so I simply gazed out at the scenery rolling by.

The thing that I noticed first of all, and the one thing I found somewhat odd, was the repetitiveness of the color scheme of most of the houses and buildings in Holland. Almost every structure we passed seemed to be made out of dark brown bricks, with an orange or dark blue tile roof. Occasionally there would be a white building or some other color combination, but it seemed like nearly 90% of the homes, stores, offices and other structures we passed fell into the brown brick/orange or blue roof category. In all honesty, I didn't find this color scheme particularly appealing, but I mostly thought it was very surprising that a people who seemed to pride themselves on their artistic contributions to this planet were so mundane when it came to their own surroundings. But, hey, it's their country, I thought. Who cares what color the buildings are?

When we got to the modest, one story house on *Bischop Bekkerslaan*, we grabbed our suitcases and walked in through the front door, and Pippi the "wonder dog" was there to greet us. She was a small "Boeren Fox," or "Farmer's Fox Terrier," a breed I was not familiar with, and she made sure she let everyone know that someone was coming into the house. After about 10 minutes of continuous barking, Pippi finally quieted down and I met Yo's father, Piet for the second time. Piet had visited us in Long Beach one day during a vacation in America the summer before. He wasn't unfriendly to me, but I can't honestly say he was particularly friendly either. He didn't seem to mind that I was there, but he wouldn't be at all upset if I wasn't either. On top of that he didn't speak very much English as a rule, so he and I never had too much to say to each other. At first I thought he might be a little put out about my being there, but I soon came to know that that was simply his personality, and according to Yo, I was trying to "read too much" into things—again!

Yo's parents had set up two twin mattresses for us to sleep on in one of the spare bedrooms. We spent about an hour showing them some pictures of our travels in America and my daughters. Then we had some soup and something hot to drink, and by this time we realized we had both been traveling non-stop for well over 24 hours, and it was definitely time to crash—so we did! We both stumbled into the spare bedroom and slept for over 12 hours until we had the energy to get up and try to figure out what to do next.

THE EMBASSY GAME

Chapter XI

T he next day was a Sunday, and it turned out to be "Meet the Wassenbergs" Day. I got to meet Yo's brother, Bart, his girlfriend/wife, Desiree, their two kids, and Yo's sisters, Trudie and Maaike (pronounced *Mike—ah*). They were all friendly enough and they all spoke English very well, so I was able to have a relatively significant conversation with all of them. However, I found out that although many Dutch people understand and can speak English, since it isn't their first language, they quickly go back to Dutch when they are talking amongst themselves. As a result, I tended to spend quite a bit of time sitting and listening, trying to follow conversations in a language I didn't understand. Unfortunately, I didn't have very much success, but I did pick up bits and pieces of what was going on during the short "translation periods" I would get from time to time.

One of Yo's sisters, and at first, also her mother felt that Yo had been extremely foolish to stay in the U.S. after her passport had expired. Yo explained to them, very patiently, that the passport expiration was not the reason she had been deported. The fact that she had overstayed her temporary visa by almost 5 years was the reason why she had been sent back. For some reason, this seemed to be more acceptable to them! In any event, after Yo and the rest of the family got caught up on what everyone had been doing for the last five years, we had a big Chinese dinner and collapsed into bed again shortly after everyone had left.

The next day was the day we were going to the U.S. embassy in Amsterdam. The night before, I had taken the three sets of applications for Yo's visa reinstatement and waiver of penalties for overstaying her visa, etc., etc., which Margaret Parker had prepared for us before I left. Yo's mother drove us back to the train station in Oss and we got on the train to Amsterdam.

We got to the central train station in Amsterdam (the Centraal Station) right about noon, which gave us time to find something to eat and catch the street trolley to the embassy near the Museumplein (Museum Square), before the 1:30 p.m. entrance time. We took the trolley to the intersection closest to the address we had gotten over the internet.

Once we got there, we were a little surprised by the long line of people standing outside the embassy's wrought iron railing fence. Apparently, there were a lot of people that needed to obtain or renew a visa to allow them to enter the United States!

The embassy hours for immigration issues were only from 1:30 p.m. to 3:30 p.m. on Mondays, Tuesdays and Thursdays, so we wanted to make sure we got inside before 3:30. However, the long line that we had to stand in was moving so slowly that we began to worry that we might not make it inside in time. Maybe I should say *I* began to worry, because Yo, as always, didn't really worry about anything. The line seemed to creep along and we finally got to the point where we had to empty our pockets and let a security guard run a metal detector all along our bodies before we were allowed to enter the building.

At about 2:45 P.M. the guard inside the main entrance buzzed us through the door from behind his safety window. Once inside, we were told to go to window # 6. We passed through a waiting room into a smaller room with six windows facing out from the far wall, like a series of old fashioned bank teller windows. Once again we had to wait in line for ten or fifteen minutes until it was our turn to take care of business.

When I got to the front of the line I looked at the name badge on the blouse of the woman on the other side of the window. Amazingly enough, it was the same woman I had spoken to the two or three times I had called the embassy from America—*Vivian Wyatt*! The same Vivian Wyatt who sounded very Dutch over the phone and who also sounded very unsympathetic—some might even say "snotty"—to me when I called to try to find out how long we could expect this whole process to take. Miss Wyatt seemed to be particularly delighted to tell me that no one could predict how long it might take Yolande to have her visa reinstated to allow her to return to the U.S., or even *IF* she would have her visa reinstated. If I wanted to accompany Yolande to the embassy and submit the application forms that needed to be submitted, that was up to me, Miss Wyatt told me, *very* pointedly, but there was no guarantee she would be allowed to return to the U.S. and even if she was, there was no way of telling how long it might take.

I had been warned by Margaret Parker and also by our contact at the Dutch consulate before I left the U.S. that I might encounter this type of attitude at the embassy. They had absolutely no incentive to be friendly or helpful to us, they warned me, so don't be surprised if they try to make everything as difficult as possible.

Miss Wyatt definitely seemed to be determined to live up to this perception. She immediately recognized my name as I slid the paperwork Margaret Parker had prepared for us through the slot under the window that separated us.

"Oh, Mr. Durack!" she said. "I remember talking to you on the phone! So you are here from America to try to reinstate your wife's visa, is that right?"

I told her that was correct. She then quickly glanced over the application form I had given her and all of the attachments that went with it, including the pictures of Yo and me at various places all over the U.S. during the past two years, which Margaret had told me to include in order to show that we didn't get a "quickie" marriage.

After studying the form and its attachments for all of 15 seconds, Vivian looked at me and asked, "And where are the certified copies of your divorce papers?"

I stood there and stared at her for a few seconds because I wasn't sure exactly what I should say. Margaret Parker had told me I would need copies of my divorce decrees to be attached to the visa reinstatement application form, and I had copies of each of my two divorce decrees attached, just like she told me. But she never told me anything about having _certified_ copies of my divorce papers!

I looked at Vivian Wyatt waiting for me to give her an answer. I said, "Nobody told me I would need _certified_ copies of my divorce decrees!" but we both knew what was coming next.

"Yes, Mr. Durack, I'm sorry, but if you had read the requirements for the visa reinstatement application on our website, you would have known that this was a requirement for the application." I had read the information on the website, but there was so much legalese involved, I thought I was safe in having Margaret prepare the forms and just follow her instructions—after all, _she_ was the immigration lawyer!

Vivian even remembered that I had told her I was self employed when I had talked to her on the phone, because she had cautioned me about leaving my job to come to Holland and try to personally submit the visa reinstatement application with Yo (even though that's what Margaret recommended). She knew that I had a couple of home based businesses which were my primary sources of income at that time.

"I hope you didn't sell all your business equipment, Mr. Durack!" she said, ever so sweetly.

Maybe she was actually trying to sound sympathetic, but for some reason it just sounded like she was trying to get my goat, like she was mentally sticking out her tongue at me and saying "I told you so! I told you so!" to herself. I felt like I had to tell her that I wasn't _that_ big of a fool, so I said, "No, I work out of my house, so I didn't have anything that I had to sell!"

"Well, I'm sorry," she said as she handed back the paperwork to me, looking very pleased with herself, I thought. "You'll have to get certified copies of your divorce papers before you can submit this." I felt like my face had to be turning bright pink by then, so I just took the forms back from her and walked away.

Certified copies! Why didn't Margaret tell me that?? I couldn't believe I had more paperwork to deal with and that I would now have to get it from the Los Angeles County and San Diego County court systems! I didn't know exactly how long that might take but I had a bad feeling that it was going to be longer than the 12 weeks I had planned on spending in Holland. I looked at Yo and tried to think of something to say to ease the disappointment. As usual, I didn't have to worry about her. "Oh well," she said, "I guess we'll just have to wait until you can get the certified copies from America."

Of course! To her, it was no big deal. To me, it was another major oversight that I wanted to kick myself for, for relying on someone else to guide us through the maze of forms and regulations involved in getting this taken care of. The only good thing about it was that Yo was taking it all in stride, and I knew that even though it might now take twice as long as we had expected, she still wouldn't be discouraged no matter what happened.

We walked outside the embassy together and got my briefcase back from the security guards. "I'm sorry," I said to her, but of course, she simply shrugged her shoulders and said "Hey, no big deal! We just have to wait a little longer that's all!"

Of course she was absolutely right again. But I started to wonder just how much longer it would take as we boarded the street car to go back to the Centraal Station and take the train back to Uden.

PLEASE TRY AGAIN LATER

Chapter XII

Y o and I spent the next two weeks visiting various tourist attractions in Holland. We went to the Arnhem open air museum, which had exhibits of early farm life and buildings in the Netherlands. We also took a bus tour to go up to Volendam, a fishing village in the North of Holland. We also took a trip to the Dutch version of Disneyland called Da Efteling. It was quite a bit smaller of course, but was based on the same principle: a family oriented amusement park with lots of pretty flowers, gardens and statues, rides and displays geared mainly towards kids. After each trip we would return to her parents' house in Uden and sack out on the mattresses in our temporary bedroom.

The schedule at her parents' house started to get pretty routine. Yo's mom cooked and served dinner every night at almost exactly 7:00 p.m. If you were there then you got fed, if not, you didn't. Yo, Rieke, Piet and I would sit at the dinner table every night to eat. Yo and Rieke had dinner conversations in Dutch, occasionally saying something to me in English to give me something to do. I felt like I now understood how most family dogs must feel. Whenever they switched from Dutch to English, they would say something like, "Isn't that right, Mike? The Beatles went all over America right?" I probably reacted the same way a dog might react when someone called his name and said something like, "Isn't that right, Sparky? You like to go for rides in the car, right?"

Piet would sit down, eat everything on his plate, wait for his vanilla "vla"(a kind of soupy pudding) to be served for dessert, and the *second* he finished that he would be up and out of his chair—without ever saying one word! The first time this happened I thought it was very strange and wondered if maybe he was just in a bad mood that night. Soon I came to realize that I was the only one who thought any of this was strange. Neither Yo nor Rieke ever batted an eye at this, so I figured it must just be me.

After dinner, I would walk Pippi. Yo helped her mom do the dishes and Piet settled into his chair in the living room to watch TV. Around 8:30 or so, Riekke would go off to watch TV in her own bedroom while Piet stayed up watching TV in the living room until 2:00 a.m. or later. Yo and I would go off to bed around midnight, and that's the way it went day in, day out with very few variations.

To my big surprise, I was the early bird in the house! I usually got up around 7:00 a.m. or 7:30 at the latest, and I assumed that Piet and Riekke would be up ahead of me (my experience with living with my ex-in-laws for short times led me to believe that anyone older than me was an early riser.) It turned out that I was usually up two to three hours ahead of anyone else. Since most of the TV shows were in Dutch, and I didn't have a car to drive anywhere, and I didn't feel like walking around town, trying to stumble along with my primitive Dutch phrases, I would usually make coffee and play chess on the internet.

After the end of the first week, Yo and I both realized that it really didn't make a lot of sense for me to stay in Holland with nothing to do until the copies of my divorce papers came through, so I started making plans to go back to America to earn some more money. I started searching for affordable air fares on the internet and finally found a few. I decided to go back for a few weeks or until I received the certified copies of my divorce papers. Obviously, this whole process was going to take a bit longer than 12 weeks after all!

I sent out a few emails to friends and acquaintances asking if they had any part time or temporary jobs I might be able to fill when I came back, but didn't get any bites. About two weeks after I arrived, Yo and I made the trip back to Schiopol airport. She kissed me goodbye, wished me luck and watched me board the plane back to America. It felt very strange to be going back after two weeks when it had taken me so long to find out when she was going to be sent to Holland, and how long I had waited to be with her during those seven weeks while she was in El Paso.

But now we had to wait for more paperwork to satisfy the bureaucratic process. I got on the plane and hoped that the next time I returned to Holland would be the final leg of the journey.

I obviously didn't realize it at the time, but we were just getting warmed up.

IF AT FIRST YOU DON'T SUCCEED....

Chapter XIII

I got back to America and started wondering what I was going to do until I could get certified copies of my divorce papers and go back. I came back to the room that Yo and I had been renting from Cyn in her house in Long Beach and started looking for a temporary job.

I was looking in the want ads for any kind of job that I didn't think I would have to make a long term commitment to. I even went to a job fair for an air freight company that was hiring customer service representatives for their night shifts. It was out at L.A. Airport, which meant it would take me at least 40 minutes to get there without any major traffic, and it wasn't the kind of pay I was used to from my full time accounting jobs. Still, it was something I could do to earn at least a little money before I went back to Holland—whenever that would be. I went through the interview process and apparently passed because I was told I would get a call advising me about what shift I would be reporting to work for the following week. I started driving to the medical clinic to get my pre-employment "physical" out of the way (aka pissing in a paper cup for a drug test) when I though about calling Burt.

Burt had been my boss at my last "real job" as an Assistant Controller for a division of a large multi-national aerospace company. He had come in to replace the previous Vice President of Finance who had left the company shortly after I started there. He was a very serious, short, no-nonsense kind of guy who really believed that keeping the financial records straight and accurate was one of life's highest callings. He was almost the total opposite of me when he came to take over the department I worked in, but I did my best to keep my irreverence under control and play the part of the dedicated company man.

The problem I had was that, by that time in my life, I really didn't like Accounting, and creating financial statements was pretty boring to me. I had wanted to do something else with my life for a long, long time, but I could never find anything else I could do that paid as well as Accounting, and I was never in a position to make less money than I was already making.

When I started working at the division of the aerospace company, I found out that it was such a large, massive, worldwide company that everyone who worked there had gotten pigeon-holed into a very narrow specialty. Most of the people there knew a lot about doing a very limited number of things and knew absolutely nothing about what anybody else did. They even had projects that they worked on that everyone knew by the abbreviations for the names of the projects (like the "PRQ 7 project", or something similar), but they didn't know what the project was actually *FOR*.

This wasn't all that unusual in this division however, because for the most part, the company did computer programming work. They didn't need to know what the project was supposed to be for, they just needed to know what programs they were supposed to write and what the programs were supposed to do. Still, I thought it was a little bit strange when people would tell you that the PRQ 7 project would have to be pushed back a year, and when you asked them what the PRQ 7 project actually was, they would just shrug their shoulders and move on to the next abbreviation.

What was even more unusual about my job was that I quickly discovered during the first few weeks that, aside from the monthly reporting duties, I had almost *nothing* to do every day!

I had 7 people that reported to me, but they were always so deeply entrenched in their own jobs that when I asked them if I could help them with anything, they couldn't even explain to me how they did their reports or where they got their information. The accounting system had been designed so that only the people who actually worked on certain reports could access the files with the information they used, so trying to help out by working on any of their files with them became very difficult. When Burt arrived, he seemed to be more comfortable talking directly to the people who reported to me, rather than meeting with me and telling me what he wanted done, and allowing me to delegate the work to the people under me.

At first I resented this, but after a while I realized he was going to do it this way whether I liked it or not, and he didn't seem to hold me accountable for anything that was or wasn't done, so I decided to just go along with it. Besides, I wasn't really eager to take on more accounting reports anyway, because I was hoping that someday soon I would be able to leave them behind altogether. I decided to try to keep myself busy with the few monthly reports I was asked to do and not rock the boat. This seemed to work out fine with Burt—or at least I thought so until our annual "review meeting", in which he told me he did not think I was "suited for senior management" at the company and wouldn't be moving any further up the ladder there.

Although he was definitely right, (by this time I had _no_ aspirations to be a senior manager in that company or any others), I was more than a little insulted to be given such an assessment, and I told him so. However, it actually helped me realize that it was time to branch out and try to find a different way to earn a living after all these years.

I decided to give Burt my notice of termination. To my surprise, he kept asking me to delay my departure until the company could find a replacement for me or to re-structure the department. I kept revising my departure date until at least 6 months had passed from the time I had initially planned to quit. To make a long story short, Burt and I had never been the best of friends during our time together, but we did actually part on very good terms once I told him I wouldn't be staying on any longer. I think it was actually a relief for both of us.

Even though we had left on better terms than when we had met each other, I was a little hesitant to call him and ask him if he had any temporary work I might be able to do before I had to go back to Holland. However, when I called him I was amazed to hear him say he had a temporary record retention project I could work on. I met him at his office the next week and he explained the project to me.

This was an extremely tedious, boring cataloging project that I would have to do at a remote records storage warehouse—but it paid $25.00 per hour! Two weeks at that would earn me nearly three thousand dollars, which would be a nice addition to my bank account and give me some more funds to survive on when I went back to Europe! I called Yolande and told her my good fortune. I think she was almost as surprised as I was, but of course she would never let on.

I spent the next two weeks cataloging records in a windowless room in a warehouse in Buena Park, California. The only breaks I got were calling my daughter Amanda in San Diego County to ask her to go to the courthouse to get the certified copies of my divorce from her mother. (I had already received the certified copies of my divorce in L.A. County.)

At first she was reluctant to go, simply because she wasn't sure what to ask for or how to deal with the civil servant mentalities in the courthouse. She even went once after I had made arrangements with one of the clerks there to have a certified copy waiting at the desk for her. However, the desk clerk had one of those nasty, hostile attitudes, much like Vivian Wyatt in Holland, and wouldn't help her get them. I told her to have them send them to her address in Oceanside, because I had spoken to Yolande on the phone and since we now knew we would have the certified copies we needed, we had decided I would be returning to Holland at the end of three weeks.

Amanda eventually got the divorce papers, but I wanted to get back to see Yo as soon as possible. She had decided that once I came back, that we were not going to sit in her parents' house doing nothing for the 12 weeks the process was supposed to take—so she made some plans for us. She went to a travel agency in Holland and booked trips to England, Ireland, France, Italy and the Czech Republic! I was amazed she was able to find trips cheap enough to all these places so that we could afford to go! But she told me they were all bus tours and that we would be the youngest ones on the bus and definitely would not be staying at four star hotels.

This was all fine with me. I made arrangements for my return flight and told Amanda how to get the divorce papers to me once they arrived. I couldn't believe I was actually going to see all those places I had only read about or seen in movies! It sure sounded better than sitting around her parents' house in Holland for 12 weeks! Maybe this whole adventure wasn't going to be that terrible after all!

Lunch in New Mexico the day before the fateful trip to White Sands

The infamous White Sands National Monument

Yo with Mogens and Ria and some fellow Dutch travelers in
Piccadilly Circus, London.

The human bone pyramid in the church at Kutna Hora
(before the train ride!)

Overlooking an Amsterdam canal
on the way to the Embassy.

Relaxing by the Cliffs of Moher in Ireland.

On the bus with the ouwetjes. I'm the one under 75, third row on the right.

At Da Efteling, the Dutch version of Disneyland

Sight seeing outside the
Tower of London

Back in the U.S. of
A.—15 months and
10 countries after
the visit to a "National
Monument".

TRAVELING WITH THE OUWETJES

Chapter XIV

I flew back to Holland on Saturday, April 28th, one day after my birthday. During my stopover in Philadelphia, I called my daughter Marilyn in Wisconsin to use my cell phone one last time before I was "unreachable" in Europe. I remember telling her that she was the last person I was going to talk to in the United States for some time. She told me to keep in touch, and I told her I would be sending her emails and pictures of all the places I would be visiting.

Before I left I drove down to Oceanside, where my ex-wife and her husband lived. They had graciously invited me to spend the night at their house before I left for the airport in San Diego the next morning, and also let me leave my car there while I was in Europe. Leaving it at Long Beach would have been a little awkward because I had to park it on the street and it had to be moved from one side of the street to the other twice a week to avoid getting a ticket for blocking the street cleaner. When I got to John and Karen's house, Karen surprised me by giving me a St. Christopher's medal to wear while I was on my various trips. "Don't you get lost over there!" she laughed as she gave me the medal. I told her not to worry, but before I returned I would find myself in a situation where I could have used some guidance from St. Christopher or any other saint that was interested in helping me out.

Fortunately, this time there were no problems to report on my trans-Atlantic crossing. Other than being somewhat bored during the nine hour flight from Philadelphia to Amsterdam there were no major mishaps. Of course, I still only got about two hours' sleep because I never mastered the art of sleeping on a plane. I can do it almost anywhere else, except in the air. Luckily, I was coherent enough to be able to claim my baggage and find Yo waiting for me at the arrivals area.

We did the obligatory kiss, kiss, hug, hug routine and then got down to business. One of the things that surprised me at first about Yo was how businesslike she could be in situations where most people tend to get more emotional. One of the reasons we seem to be so right for each other is that neither of us gets overly sentimental or emotional when there is something that needs to be done. I'm actually more of a softie than she is in that respect, which often surprises people. It definitely does not mean we love each other more or less than any other couple. We just seem to be perfectly fine knowing it without having to make a big show of it for anyone else. We find ways to make each other happy without anyone else seeing it.

Anyway, back to the journey back to Holland. I arrived there the morning of April 30th and the next day we were getting on a bus heading for London! We stayed at Yo's parents' house the night after I arrived and the next day, Yo's mom drove us to the bus station in Oss.

Yo had warned me that we would probably be the youngest people on the bus tour and I soon found out she wasn't kidding. "Bus travel is for the ouwetjes in Europe," she told me. (Ouwetjes is pronounced "ow-itch-es", and it's the Dutch word for "older people"—kind of like "old fogies" in English.) But, since this was definitely the cheapest way to travel throughout Europe, she had booked trips for us to London, Paris, Prague and Italy while I was gone, and the London trip was the first one in the bunch.

At this point, I have to tell you a little bit about Dutch people from an ignorant American's viewpoint (mine). Once they get to know you, they are very friendly and the ones who can speak English are very outgoing and conversational. But until you get to that point, they are a little bit of what I would call "standoffish." They are not exactly unfriendly, but they don't really go out of their way to make you feel welcome either. It's not something they actually try to do. They just seem to have a very practical, unemotional outlook on life, for the most part.

This was a little bit difficult for me to get used to because I myself have been something of an introverted, non emotional kind of person for most of my life, too. In my case it started when I was a kid and had two horrendous appendages for ears sticking out from the sides of my head. I used to think "Big Ears" was my real name until I was thirteen or fourteen. Whenever I walked down the street in my cousins' neighborhood in Chicago, or anywhere outside of my home neighborhood, I would hear one of the other kids yell, "Hey, Big Ears!" out to me, and I would desperately try to find a hole to crawl into. Occasionally, some of the kids in these "foreign" neighborhoods would decide it might be fun to gang up on this big eared kid and give him a few punches in the mouth.

Needless to say, this kept me from becoming particularly outgoing until my head grew larger and eventually made my ears look normal sized. Learning to play football in eighth grade also seemed to help keep the bullies at bay. It wasn't until midway through high school, however, that I would develop enough self confidence to talk to people I didn't know without fearing ridicule or embarrassment.

I ultimately overcame my shyness and actually became a business manager as well as an amateur actor, giving speeches at business meetings and performing theatrical plays and musicals in front of live audiences. From all outward appearances, I'm sure most people would never know I ever had any problem talking to people or feeling comfortable with new people or new situations. But deep down, it still takes me a while to warm up to people and I usually don't say too much to anyone until I'm sure I'm with people who are friendly and trustworthy.

Well, the problem with someone like me being the only non-Dutch speaking person on a tour bus in Holland is that the Dutch people have this attitude that basically says "We don't care who you are, until we get to know you, we don't particularly want to talk to you, and if you don't like us, you can go back to wherever the hell you came from since we never asked you to come here in the first place." So when you're a little bit standoffish to begin with, and don't even speak the official language of the people you're traveling with, it gets a little difficult to establish many warm and fuzzy friendships. Don't get me wrong—it's not that the Dutch people are rude or hostile or even unfriendly in any way. They just don't see any need to make you feel welcome if they don't know who you are. Even after they get to know you, they don't really roll out the welcome mat, so you have to get used to very tiny bits of polite conversation on the rare occasions they decide they don't mind talking to you in English. There are exceptions, of course, but for the most part, that was the attitude I seemed to find among the ouwetjes on the bus.

So, on the morning of May 1st, 2006 I found myself on a bus with Yo and about 40 ouwetjes driving off to cross under the English Channel and continue on to London. Every once in a while one or two of the seniors on the bus would give us a look that seemed to say "What the hell are you doing here?" but for the most part nobody paid much attention to us. We made about four stops to pick up more passengers in Holland and then headed west through Belgium and France. After about five hours we came to the town of Calais, which was the entrance to the world famous "Chunnel."

The "Chunnel" is an underground tunnel between England and France that thousands of cars and buses use each day. The name "Chunnel" is an abbreviation for Channel Tunnel—hence the name "Chunnel." The interesting part of the trip is getting loaded on the train that takes you through to the other side. Our bus drove into a large train car and lined up behind other buses, cars and trucks that were all queued up for the trip to England. The train car was just wide enough to accommodate the bus and leave about six feet of space on either side. Once we were settled in line, the bus driver turned off the engine and also the air conditioning. We soon found out that not having air conditioning beneath the English Channel made for a very warm 45 minute trip!

In addition, whether you stayed inside the bus or got out to walk to the nearest bathroom or look out the train windows, there was really nothing to see. Outside the windows was nearly pitch black with an occasional maintenance sign, fire extinguisher or handrail whizzing by. The only way you could really tell you were moving was from the gentle swaying of the bus inside the train car, or from the train car itself as it sped along under the Channel. We spent a rather boring 45 or 50 minutes until we got to the other side and drove up onto the shores of England!

My first impression of England was that it looked quite a bit like the U.S. except for the fact that everyone drove on the wrong side of the road. As we got closer to London, the traffic got heavier and more congested until it felt like we were driving into New York City or Los Angeles during rush hour. We finally got to our hotel around 6:00 p.m. and checked into our room overlooking the Thames. Then we rushed downstairs to get some sightseeing in before dark and find a place to eat.

Yolande had assured me that we wouldn't have to stay on the tours with the ouwetjes, because they were usually too slow, and took too long listening to the tour guide about mundane details of whatever they were looking at and that we could make much better time on our own. Also, since she had traveled all around Europe and Turkey on her own before, she was totally confident that we could use her tour book maps and get to wherever we wanted to go using the city's subways and buses. It sounded good to me. Besides I wouldn't know what to say to the ouwetjes even if they did speak English, which they didn't seem to do very much, so I was all for us splitting off on our own.

The first thing we did was ask the desk clerk how to get to the nearest subway that would take us into downtown London. He gave us our directions and we were out the door. But first we decided that we should find an ATM so that we could get some money in English pound sterling notes. (Holland and most of the rest of the European Union used the Euro as their currency. Only England and a few other countries in Europe used something different.) So we found an ATM machine right near the bridge that we would be walking over to cross the Thames on our way to the subway station.

As we were getting our money from the ATM machine, we noticed that four other people from our bus were walking up to the same spot. The first two people were a woman in her mid forties and her daughter in her early teens. They both said something to Yolande in Dutch and she told them where we were going and what we planned on doing for dinner, etc. While she was talking to the woman and her daughter in Dutch, an older man and woman came walking up behind them. They were also from our bus and they also asked us where we were going.

At some point I think I said something in English to Yolande while she was talking to our four fellow travelers and as soon as I did, the man smiled at me and said. "You speak English?" I said yes and he seemed overjoyed. 'Where are you from?" he asked.

"America," I said.

"Where in America?"

"California, near Los Angeles."

"Oh, yes, of course," he said. "We lived in San Diego for three years!"

All of a sudden I was having a conversation with someone from Holland who didn't seem to mind speaking English! His wife heard us talking and she started talking to me and Yo in English too.

Their names were Mogens and Ria and although they lived in Holland, he was actually from Denmark and did not speak much Dutch. He just felt like he could speak Danish and English and that was enough. Ria was Dutch, but she spoke Dutch, English and Danish too, I assumed. But in any event, it was nice to meet someone besides Yo that I could actually have a conversation with. They asked if they could join us on our excursion into downtown London and we said of course. So all six of us started walking across the bridge to get to the subway station, with Yo leading the way.

Yo really was great at finding her way around—not only in London, but just about every where we went. On top of being able to read the maps and also being able to understand at least partially almost any European language, she also had, and still has, extremely good vision. She can pick out a subway sign or street sign and read it faster than I can even see the sign. In addition to this, she was a natural leader. If a group of people were standing around saying, "Gee what should we do? I don't know where to go," she would usually take that as her cue to take charge and start giving directions.

That's exactly what she did in this case, and it was really great having her as our leader. She was always confident she could find her way around, and never even imagined that she might get lost or find herself stuck in a dangerous part or town, or that anything bad could happen. As long as she could read a map or subway sign and ask directions, she felt like she could go anywhere, whether she had ever been to that place before or not.

The only trouble with this was that, because Yo was *so* confident about where she was going and what was the best course to follow, that she seldom, if ever, asked anyone else if they had any other ideas. Usually nobody did, of course, because they were like I am the first time I'm in a strange city. I just follow someone else if they seem to know where they're going and what they should do. Usually this worked out fine, but in this particular case, Mogens and Ria were quite a bit older than the rest of the group and they were having a hard time keeping up with Yo's energetic pace. Hell, even *I* was having a hard time keeping up with her pace. Yo would have made a good drill sergeant in the Marines. Her philosophy was, follow me, don't ask any questions and don't fall behind if you know what's good for you.

This was alright if we were only walking for short distances, but the London subway system has ten or twelve different levels of tunnels with escalators going up and down for miles underground. I noticed Mogens and Ria were falling farther and farther behind, but that Yo was not slowing down her pace one millisecond to make sure everyone in the group was able to stay with her. I finally had to literally *run* ahead to catch up with her and ask her to slow down for Mogens and Ria's sake (and also my own).

She seemed very surprised that anyone would think she was walking fast. To her, this was just her normal pace, but as I tried to explain to her many times, a lot of people, *like me,* did not see the need to "walk" anywhere as quickly as she did when you didn't really know where you were going in the first place, and didn't see the need to try to break any records. She actually did try to slow down somewhat but her natural instinct was to fly through crowded streets and subways as fast as possible in order to get somewhere in the shortest possible time. This would be one of the very few problems we would have traveling together, since I don't see informational signs as quickly or as clearly as she does, and I was also not accustomed to rushing from one place to another. She finally slowed down the pace so all the ouwetjes—Mogens, Ria and *me*—could keep up with her. I don't think she liked it, but she did it.

We ended up taking the subway to Piccadilly Circus, taking a few pictures on the street and going to an Indian restaurant for dinner. The next day we rode on the tour bus while it went through the shopping district, around Buckingham Palace, Westminster Cathedral and the Albert Hall. Then we took off on our own to visit the Tower of London. We spent most of the day there and found our way back to our hotel on the subway again, mostly due to Yo's expert guidance.

The next day we continued our sightseeing expedition by visiting Madame Tussaud's wax museum and taking another subway to the St. John's Wood station to visit the spot on Abbey Road that the Beatles walked across for the cover of their record album by the same name. I was a little surprised that there wasn't any plaque or any sign of any sort marking the spot as a historical place. I even had to ask an American girl who was taking pictures of the cross walk if this was the actual spot where the picture had been taken. She assured me that it was, and it sure looked like the street where John, Paul, George and Ringo walked across for their 1969 album cover, so I assumed she was right.

I wanted to have my picture taken crossing the street in the same place that the Beatles crossed in the picture. The only trouble was there wasn't any traffic light or stop sign anywhere around that crossing, so you had to wait until there weren't any cars coming in either direction. This seemed to take forever, and then when it did happen, I had to run out into the middle of the street, have Yo take my picture and run back before any more cars came by. I didn't want to get a ticket from the London police for obstructing traffic! She got one picture of me in the middle of the cross walk, but I wanted a closer shot to look more like the shot on the album cover. Since Yo had never seen the album cover, she didn't know exactly what I wanted, but got another shot of me in the road after waiting again for more cars to pass by. This still wasn't exactly what I wanted, but by this time it was getting late in the day, more and more cars kept coming by without a break in traffic, so I decided it wasn't worth waiting any longer for the perfect shot. We ended up with two shots of me in Abbey Road which turned out to be just fine, after all.

The next day we took a subway and a bus to the replica of Shakespeare's Globe Theater and saw part of a rehearsal for Shakespeare's *Coriolanus*. By this time, we barely saw anyone from the tour bus during the day, and that was fine by us. We would just keep going to see the things we wanted to see and get back in time to make sure we caught the bus back to Holland.

That night we went to a restaurant called "The Sherlock Holmes Inn" which looked like an old fashioned English Pub from the outside. The downstairs part *was* a pub, but the upstairs part was a restaurant. We went upstairs to order dinner and were seated in a dining room with only two or three other couples. We waited for what seemed like a good fifteen minutes before the waitress even came over to take our order. By this time, I was tempted to leave, but Yo always had infinite patience for waiters or waitresses and would get very annoyed with me if I even grumbled about slow service. So I decided to bite my tongue as we gave the waitress our order.

I was sorry I gave in so easily when it seemed to take about another twenty minutes before we got the first course of our order. For some reason, even though there was only a handful of people in the restaurant that night, the kitchen was churning out orders at a snail's pace. But we figured it would take just as long, if not longer to go somewhere else at that point, so we just endured the wait.

We had just gotten started on our main course, when two men walked in and sat down about three tables away from us. One of the men was a Brit who had obviously been drinking and was giving the waitress a hard time about getting his order. He had only been waiting about five minutes and already he was complaining! "Good luck, buddy," I thought to myself. "Better get used to it, you've got a long wait ahead of you before you'll see any food!" I thought he'd realize after a few minutes that everyone else had been waiting for their orders a long time too, and he'd shut up about it. But the longer he had to wait, the more he complained to the waitress—not exactly in a mean way, but more in a drunken smart-alecky wise guy way. I think he was actually trying to be funny, but the more he talked the more it irritated me.

After about twenty minutes of his complaining about not getting his order and that the waitress couldn't go downstairs to the bar for some reason to get him another drink, this guy actually got up and started waling around to talk to people at the other tables! He walked over to a table with two middle aged women sitting at it and asked them how long they had been waiting for their food. They told him about 30 minutes (at least I knew then that the kitchen was slow for everybody, not just us!) He started joking with them about how slow the service was and that we should all march down to the kitchen to protest how long the service took, or something like that. "Listen, pal, if you want to go down to the kitchen to protest, be my guest," I thought to myself, "but leave me the hell out of it. I've waited long enough for my dinner, I'm not going to let a screwball like you stop me now."

I kept wondering why he just didn't shut up and wait for his food like everyone else, but it seemed like he was actually having a good time talking to the other people in the restaurant. He eventually came over to talk to Yo and I, but by this time we were on our desert and I wasn't in any mood to play along with this guy's jokes. I don't remember what he said to us, but I said something like, "Sorry, we're just about finished here, so we're not going to be of much help to you." Of course, Yo was much more friendly and receptive to him than I was and I think she somehow made a joke out of how long it took to get our order. Right about then, his order and the order of the man he was sitting with finally came and he mercifully went back to his own table.

We had just gotten our bill and I was just about ready to pay, when the guy from the other table started talking to us again. This time he seemed a little more apologetic and asked us if we wanted to join them at their table! I told him we had already finished eating, and he said something like, "That's alright, just join us for a drink then, We'd really just like to talk to you since we're all here together." I was a little leery about going over to his table, but I looked at Yo and she seemed to be ready to go talk to them, so I thought, "Oh, well, what the hell..."

It turned out that the guy who had been babbling ever since he walked in was an Englishman named James and he looked like Steve Martin's twin brother. The guy he was with was an American with dark hair and glasses, and he and James were business partners. We all started talking about where we lived in the States and the American guy lived in Boston but he also lived in southern California and knew all the places that Yo and I had lived. I found out that James and the American had some sort of super successful medical technology business and they were meeting in London to make some sort of long range plans. I didn't really understand exactly what their business was all about, but it didn't matter much because pretty soon we were talking about politics in the U.S. and the U.K., how we all hated Bush and telling jokes.

Much to my surprise we ended up having a great time with these two guys. After dinner, we went downstairs to the pub section and had three or four rounds of Guineses and drinks before the bar closed down (at 11:00 p.m.!) They turned out to be two of the friendliest guys I've ever met on any trip, anywhere. James told me he was planning on running for office in the U.K. and was sure he would be elected because he said people were tired of being misled by politicians and that he was going to tell them the truth. I smiled and drank a toast to his political campaign, but I wondered what he thought he was saying that was any different that what every other political candidate said. But again, it didn't really matter. We were having fun talking to these guys and telling jokes. It sure beat sitting at the hotel and trying to talk to the ouwetjes!

After the pub closed we finally split up from James and his American friend (I'm sure he told me his name, but I'll be damned if I can remember what it was.) We took the subway back to our exit again, walked across the bridge over the Thames and into our hotel. By now, even I was getting to the point where I could wander around London without too much trouble, but of course, by now it was time to leave.

The next morning we got on the bus to go back to Holland. We caught up with Mogens and Ria again who told us about their visits to art galleries in London. (That's what they had gone there for, apparently, to see if there was any art that they wanted to invest in.) We found out that both of them were a lot different than the rest of the ouwetjes. For one thing they both had a raunchy sense of humor—especially Ria. For another thing, they totally understood our desire to travel on our own, away from the rest of the group. They basically did the same thing as we did, but they just went to different places. The rest of the people on the bus were "sheep," Ria told me—meaning they did what they were told and didn't have enough imagination to go do anything on their own. They really seemed to like me and Yo and they both spoke good English so even I could talk to them, so we got on great.

We wished them luck when we got to their stop (or as they say in Dutch: *success!),* and rode back to the last stop at Oss. Yo's mom was at the bus station to pick us up and take us back to Uden. Now we had a week to kill before we took a day trip to the VSO offices—the Volunteer Service Organization—in Utrecht, where Yo and I would apply to be volunteer workers to help people in a third world country! If we would be accepted, I would be living somewhere besides the United States for a few years at least.

I wasn't sure exactly how I would like that, but I knew that as long as I could be with Yo, everything would work out alright.

THIRD WORLD COUNTRIES, ANYONE?

Chapter XV

O nce we got back to Uden we settled into the "non-traveling" routine that we would have to follow for most of the twelve weeks that we used Yo's parents' house as our home base. In a nutshell, this meant that we didn't have a whole lot to do, and had to find ways to try to keep busy by taking short bike trips, walking into town for quickie shopping trips or for lunch, and going to the library for books in English that I could read to pass the time. In addition to that, I usually spent at least a couple of hours or more every day on the internet, sending emails, playing chess and just randomly surfing. Yo kept busy by reading, talking to her mom, (who was never at a loss for words or opinions), and looking up old friends and relatives that would allow us to visit them and stay at their homes for a few days.

No matter how much we tried to find things to do to keep busy, the truth of the matter is we were both pretty bored most of the time, waiting for our next trip to begin. This was especially true after our London trip because our next bus tour, to Prague, did not leave until May 21st, a whole 16 days after our return from London. Even though Yo did her best to find activities to keep us both busy, the monotony would eventually get to both of us and for the first time, we found ourselves becoming irritated with each other over silly things and getting into stupid, petty arguments. So we were both looking forward to the next big "break" in our routine, which would be the VSO interview in Utrecht on May 12th.

VSO stands for Volunteer Service Organization and it is an international entity dedicated to improving the lives of people in third world countries by providing teachers, doctors, nurses and business people from Europe, Canada and occasionally, the United States who sign up for two to four year assignments in these countries. It functions pretty similarly to the Peace Corps in the U.S., but while the Peace Corps requires any of its volunteer workers to be American citizens, the VSO doesn't care where you come from, or what your citizenship is, as long as you have the skills that they feel are needed. (Why the Peace Corps insists that all its members are U.S. citizens is beyond me, but then a lot of what our government does is beyond me—including our immigration laws. But I'll get into that much later.)

Anyway, Yo had told me about the VSO long before we took our fateful trip to White Sands and how she had always wanted to participate in it by teaching or otherwise working to improve the lives of people in third world countries. When she first started talking to me about it, I thought it was basically one of those naïve "do-gooder" type charity organizations that liked people to believe they were doing some good in the world, but were really just putting temporary "band aids" on the huge bleeding hemorrhages in the poor places of the planet. However, the more she told me about it, and the more I looked into it, the more I thought it might be one way I could actually do something meaningful in my life. After all, I had never been a huge success in either the business world, or in the entertainment arena, so I thought maybe I could make a difference by helping someone else improve their lives. It took a little getting used to, but I eventually came to realize that, if we could both be accepted, working for the VSO for a few years could well be the most significant thing I would do in my lifetime. I decided to take the first step in the application process and schedule a conference call for me and Yo in December of 2005.

We started by sending an email to the VSO headquarters in Canada. We really wanted to apply through the office in Holland, but the website stated that all North American residents had to apply through the Canadian office. We then received an email back advising us as to when a conference call would be arranged for both Yolande and me to discuss what type of lifestyle we would experience if we were selected to join VSO, monetary and physical hardships that we might have to endure, and our overall psychological compatibility for a long term assignment in a foreign culture.

The conference call took place a few days before Christmas in 2005. Yo and I were both living in Cynthia's house at the time and we had two extension phones available so that we could both listen to the VSO representative who called us. The phone interview seemed to go well, and when we explained that we both desired an assignment somewhere outside of North America, we were told that we would have to send an application to the VSO European headquarters in Holland. Little did we know at the time that we would both be in Holland within the next four months, and would be able to apply there in person.

So now, here we were in Holland, ready to go to the VSO interview in Utrecht on the morning of May 12th. We both had copies of our diplomas and had filled out the application forms they had sent us, so we got up early to get a ride to the train station in Oss from Yo's mom and headed out to Utrecht, about an hour away.

We got to the Utrecht train station early, so we walked around the town for about a half hour, taking in the 17th century buildings and churches, which were really old hat to Yo, but were still pretty interesting to me. We took a few pictures at one of the local churches and finally walked over to the VSO office.

We were a little early and did not find anyone inside when we walked through the door. The office was actually on the second floor above some kind of engineering or business services office on the first floor. Since I couldn't read very much Dutch, I couldn't read their signs and didn't know what kind of office it was, but luckily, Yolande could and she found out from the receptionist where the VSO office was.

When we got to the top of the stairs we found two other people who were applying that day, a young couple in their twenties. We said hello, and they quickly determined that I had to be an American or English, so they kindly spoke to us in English. He was an engineer of some sort and she was a doctor who had just finished medical school. They hadn't established any kind of regular jobs yet, so this was the ideal time for them to try to join VSO. We told them our stories and waited for the official administrative type people to show up.

Two more applicants showed up within the next fifteen minutes, both females. One was a student who wasn't quite out of school yet and the other was a woman in her early thirties looking for a career change. I think she may have been a teacher, but don't remember for sure.

Anyway, about 9:00 a.m. the group leader walked in, introduced himself and then had us all introduce ourselves to each other, even though we had already done this informally. This time around, everyone gave the group a few more details about themselves and talked about why they wanted to work for VSO. When it came time for me and Yo to tell everyone why we wanted to apply, I said something like "I've been able to be successful in the business world and I feel like it's time I tried to give something back to help other people." That was mostly bull, but in a strange roundabout way, it was true, too.

I had tried teaching twice before at the college level and found out I didn't get any sense of reward or leadership by explaining debits and credits or how to distinguish an asset from a liability. For the most part, I felt that Accounting was pretty mundane and utilitarian by nature, and about the best thing you could say about it was that it was truly a necessary evil in the business world. But I never got any great sense of accomplishment from teaching it and thought it was almost a disservice to lead someone into that type of lifestyle—spending countless hours analyzing spread-sheets and journal entries and stressing out over month end deadlines. But then I thought that there would always be people who actually *enjoyed* doing that sort of thing, and besides, if it was something they really *wanted* to learn, I was sure I could find a way to teach them almost everything they needed to know. So, I wasn't really lying when I told the VSO group that I thought I had something to give back to anyone who actually wanted to learn accounting or bookkeeping. I just still had a hard time understanding why anyone would want to do it if they didn't have to. But since that was my area of expertise, that was all I had to offer.

Yo, on the other hand, was terrific with communicating with people on just about any subject under the sun. She was extremely outgoing and could make just about anyone feel comfortable with her in a matter of minutes. On top of that, she spoke five languages and was always interested in learning about new cultures and customs. She would be a natural at fitting in with a new group of people in a different culture and environment. I was sure that with her people skills and my formal training and background we would be approved to join VSO.

The only problem that either one of us could foresee was in the fact that Yo had absolutely no teaching experience to speak of, even though her college degree was intended specifically to teach art at the high school level. Since teaching experience was something that was highly prized by VSO, and also because she had no formal business training, Yo was skeptical of our chances from the very start. I thought that once they talked to her in person and saw what a friendly, outgoing person she was that they couldn't help but accept both of us.

We went through the obligatory question and answer routine, talking about things like how we would handle problems which could arise in a foreign "third world" country, like how to deal with a government official who was disliked by the public but necessary to maintain the VSO's operations in that country, etc. We then had to rank a series of problems from minor to significant and explain why, and what steps could be taken to overcome them. But the highlight of the day was the group activity.

We were given a task to complete as a group, which was basically to make booklets out of newspaper using specific dimensions with a limited amount of tools (scissors) and time. Of course the goal was to see if we could organize ourselves and figure out who would do what as efficiently as possible, and I believe we failed miserably. The biggest problem we had was that nobody wanted to take charge or appear to be bossy in any way. As a result, everyone just suggested different ways we might be able to complete the project with several starts and stops along the way. Yo seemed to be the only one of us capable of taking charge and giving directions to maximize the efficiency needed to get the job done on time, but it turned out that she jumped in a little too late. We were only about two thirds of the way done with getting the newspaper cut to the right dimensions and sorted the right way in order to make our booklets when we ran out of time. We then had a group review to discuss what we had done wrong and right, and everyone agreed that we were all basically just too polite to tell each other what to do.

The group leader did not give any hints as to whether or not we had demonstrated what we needed to know in order to be accepted. He simply listened while we each explained why we hadn't been able to complete the project on time, as directed, and then gave us all a non-committal farewell speech, telling us that we would receive our evaluations by mail within a few days. He ended by wishing us all well and hoped we would have continued success in our future endeavors, blah, blah, blah, blah, blah. We ended the session by finding an outdoor café within a few blocks of the VSO office and sitting down as a group for a farewell drink.

Yo and I finished our drinks, said goodbye to our fellow applicants, and got back on the train for Oss, wondering if we would find out what the next step would be in our VSO quest during the next few days. If we were to be accepted, we would be scheduled for a three day "in-depth training seminar", and then a two week "hands on" experience somewhere relatively close by, and ultimately a two to three year assignment in another country. I started wondering where we would end up, and how I would actually be able to deal with living in a primitive environment somewhere in Africa or Asia. I wasn't really worried, because I knew that as long as I was with Yo, we would find a way to work it out, no matter what happened. We had gotten through some weird times together already and we would get through more of them in the future, if we had to.

I didn't really know it then, but one of those times was going to come up very soon.

STRANDED IN KUTNA HORA

Chapter XVI

We came back to Uden and had another 9 days to wait before we left on our next trip to Prague in the Czech Republic. During that time we tried to keep busy by taking bike trips to local castles, taking pictures of the Dutch countryside, walking to town for mini-shopping trips, eating at the local restaurants and going to a movie once a week. Of course, we also spent a lot of time picking up books at the library, and when all else failed, I could always play games on the internet. Even though we knew we would have to find ways to keep busy between trips it was almost always a challenge to find enough to do, especially from my end because I didn't know anyone outside of Yo's family and couldn't hop in my car to go drive somewhere whenever I felt like it.

We waited for the requisite three days before we got the letter from VSO informing us of their decision. Incredibly enough, they accepted me but rejected Yo! I was actually amazed but Yo wasn't at all surprised. Apparently, her lack of classroom teaching experience made them think she wasn't qualified, in spite of her good performance during the evaluation meeting. I knew then, just as I know now, that the VSO missed a great opportunity to get two members who would be willing to work very hard in whatever environment they were sent to because of a technicality. They obviously chose not to overlook Yo's lack of classroom teaching experience even though she could get along with almost everyone, spoke five languages and was a natural born leader when the situation required it. I was definitely disappointed, but Yo seemed to take it all in stride, as always. So instead of complaining, we went about our daily activities, visited De Efteling, (the Dutch version of Disneyland), and waited for the next trip to come up.

On May 21, 2006, we got on the bus for the trip to Prague. Once again, we were the youngest couple on the bus, with about 40 or 45 ouwetjes to share the 9 or 10 hour ride with. The only difference on this trip was that we sat next to an older Dutch man and his wife who actually seemed to enjoy talking to us in English. Eventually, they would slip back into Dutch, especially when Yo and the wife started talking, but at least for part of the time, there was someone else on the bus besides Yo who actually talked to me without being forced to do so. We didn't sit and chat like old friends or anything, but at least he would occasionally ask, "How was your dinner?" or "Nice view, eh?" while we were riding through Germany on the way to the Czech Republic. Every once in a while, when we passed each other at a restaurant or rest stop, he would look at me and say, "Hey Joe!" like it was some sort of universal American greeting. I would just smile and say, "Hoi!" or "Goede Morgen!" back to him. It didn't really matter what he said, at least he was trying to talk to me. It probably wouldn't seem like much to most people, but it helped me feel a little less isolated.

Once we got to Prague, we checked into our hotel, which was located on the outskirts of town. As usual, Yo had read up in her guide books about all the places she thought would be fun to go to, and quickly learned how to catch a bus outside the hotel which would take us into the main part of town and the local subway system.

The subway systems in Europe are really terrific. Yo had told me that once you learned how to ride one of them, you could get around on almost any subway system there, and she was right.

The first day we were in Prague, we went to breakfast in the hotel that was provided as part of the tour, got on the bus for the ride into town with all of the ouwetjes, but once we were there, we said "Goodbye!" and went off to explore on our own, at our own pace on our own schedule.

Some of the ouwetjes always looked at us a little curiously whenever we did this, as if they were thinking, "How do they always know their way around in a strange place? What makes them so smart? Are they both travel agents when they're not on trips like this?" They never actually came out and asked us any of these questions, but you could tell they were dying to know how we were able to get around everywhere by ourselves.

It actually was pretty simple, although being able to speak at least one other language would probably have made it even easier for me. Luckily, I always had Yo to depend on. She would read the bus schedule, figure out where we should go, and all I had to do was follow her. Once we were on the bus or subway she would tell me when we would have to get off, and I soon figured out how to read the maps inside the subway cars to understand where we had to go. Yo was right, they all used the same type of universal graphics. Once you learned to read one, you could read them all in any of the European countries, at least. However, I never expected to be put to the test the way I was when we went to Kutna Hora.

Kutna Hora (pronounced Kutch-na Hore-ah) is a small town about 80 kilometers or 60 miles outside of Prague. Yo had read about it in the guidebook and thought it would be an interesting place to go see. It was supposed to have a church made almost entirely out of human bones! You know, like skulls, leg bones, arm bones, etc.! It was something that monks did in the Middle Ages because they ran out of room to bury people in the cemetery. I don't know why they couldn't just find a nice hillside to bury them in instead, but for whatever reason, they decided to save the bones of the people who died for something like 50 to 100 years and eventually built a church out of it! I had to admit this was something that was probably worth seeing, creepy as it may have been. So after we had done our sightseeing all around Prague itself on the first two days, we decided to jump off on our own and take the train to Kutna Hora.

Prague itself was actually very beautiful, by the way. The town square with the old fashioned 1600 era buildings and shops was a terrific sight and the old section of town with the medieval churches—including one that took over 250 steps to climb to the top of the highest tower (great exercise!)—were fantastic. We took quite a few pictures and had a great time exploring the castles, churches and town squares, all on our own of course. But after two days, we decided it was time to go see something different and we told the tour guide that we would be on our own that day so that we could take the train to Kutna Hora.

To get to Kutna Hora, first you had to get on the bus outside our hotel and go further into the city of Prague. After a certain point, you could get off the bus and walk around the business area to get to the subway. The subway stations were located every few blocks or so and were very easy to find. Once inside the subway station you had to buy a ticket at an automated ticket machine and get on the subway—basically the same way it works in London or Paris or any other modern European city. From there, you took the subway to the main train station and once at the main train station you boarded the train to Kutna Hora. I didn't really know how to figure any of this out myself, but Yo had done all her homework before the trip began and knew exactly what stop to get off at, where the train station was, etc., so all I had to know was how to follow her.

We took the train to Kutna Hora, which was about an hour away and just sat and relaxed by watching the passing scenery, although there was nothing really spectacular to see, but that's all there was to do anyway. Once we got to the main station for Kutna Hora, we found that you have to take a shuttle train for about another 30 miles to get right into town. Once we got there we started hiking around, looking for the sights Yo had picked out from her guide book.

In addition to the church made out of bones there were some beautiful old cathedrals to look at—every town in Europe has beautiful old cathedrals, it seems. In addition to that we also found a medieval silver mine that you could go down into for a small fee. Needless to say, we couldn't pass up this opportunity, so we both paid the admission fee and put on white coats and miners' helmets to go down into the mine. This was a medieval mine, mind you, so there weren't any modern conveniences like elevators to take you to the bottom. Instead you just walked down a winding staircase that eventually got you to the bottom of a deep dark, cavern. That's why they gave us flashlights to find our way through the narrow cavern trail, since again, there were no modern conveniences like electric lights. I'm sure there weren't any flashlights around then either, but I guess they didn't want to take the chance of some tourist setting himself on fire with a candle down there.

There were places inside that dark mine trail where I almost had to kneel down to get through, and luckily I was still able to squeeze my 225 lb. body through the narrow passages all along the route. We even were able to take some pictures down inside the mine by flashlight. They didn't come out all that well, but still, it was really a lot of fun.

We finished our mine tour and now it was time to take the bus to Kutna Hora. Before we left we ran into a Dutch couple at one of the cathedrals we were visiting. When they found out I was an

American, the man, who was in his late sixties or seventies became very friendly and talkative. He told me he really appreciated America for what we did for Europe in World War Two. I knew that the "American attitude" towards Europeans about World War Two and how we had saved their continent from the Nazis was a little bit of a sore point, so I was somewhat surprised to find a European who was out and out grateful to America. He told me he had lived in Indonesia as a child, which at that time was a Dutch colony, and at the outbreak of the war he had been taken prisoner by the Japanese, just like Yolande's mom, Rieke. He said he was forever grateful that America had dropped the bomb on Japan because that was what he felt ended the war and eventually got him released from a Japanese prison camp. I told him I was glad it happened for him, but still sorry that it had to happen at all. But then, who ever wants a war to happen to begin with?

Anyway, it was just kind of refreshing to meet a European who was that friendly and didn't act like you were supposed to apologize for being an American. Not that a lot of them did, outwardly at least, but I had heard enough stories to know that we were not looked upon as the most likable people to visit Europe. Unfortunately, a lot of Europeans judge Americans by the tourists they see, who aren't always the most gracious people. But anyway, that's another issue, and as more and more Americans begin to travel more, and learn about other cultures I think it's starting to change. At least I hope so.

After we got on the local bus and took a few wrong turns, we finally found the cathedral made out of human bones. It was truly a sight to see. It looked like a regular church building on the outside, but once you got inside you saw pyramids of human skulls and chandeliers and tables made out of skulls and human bones! The amazing part was that, even though it sounds incredibly creepy, it was actually intensely interesting. Since these were people who had just died normal deaths, and the monks weren't trying to make anything scary out of it, just trying to find a way to keep the peoples' remains in the church forever, it didn't seem spooky or creepy at all. It was actually a great place for pictures and we took our share to show everyone back home and gross them all out!

When we were ready to leave Kutna Hora we walked back to the train station, bought our tickets and waited for the next shuttle train, which was scheduled to arrive about 7:00 p.m. After we got on the train, we waited for the conductor to come around and clip our tickets to show they had been used. When he took our tickets, however, we knew something was wrong. He looked at them with a very concerned look on his face and then said something in Czech that I didn't understand, but it was clear he was telling us we were on the wrong train. Instead of going west, back to Prague, we were headed east—at least I think that's what happened. We asked him if we were going west to Prague and apparently he understood English well enough to shake his head solemnly at us. He then pointed back the opposite way from where we were going and said something about getting off at the next station and going back that way. So we waited for the train to stop about a mile or two up the track and got off.

Since there was only one track, the shuttle train was the only train going back and forth on that route all day long. Therefore, the train would not be going back in the other direction for another hour or so, so we started walking back along the train tracks towards Kutna Hora. The next train to Prague was supposed to be around 7:30 according to the train schedule so we tried to set a fairly quick pace in order to get there in time. Unfortunately, the route was through a fairly rural part of the country, and we had to walk alongside farms, thick vegetation and dirt roads most of the time, so we weren't quite fast enough. We got to the station at about 7:25 and the train had already stopped at 7:20 and left. Therefore we had about an hour and a half wait before the next shuttle train for Prague was scheduled to arrive around 9:00 p.m. Since we wouldn't get back to our hotel in time for the dinner which was included in our trip, we said, "What the heck, let's try out a restaurant in Kutna Hora!" The only alternative was to wait and try to find a place to eat that was still open around 10:00 p.m. when we got back to Prague, so it wasn't a very hard choice.

We walked to a restaurant not far from the train tracks and decided it looked okay. We opened the door and for a minute or two I thought I was back in one of the old taverns in the South Side of Chicago that I saw a few times when I was a kid. Everything looked the same—the old fashioned furniture, dark paint on the walls, the red tablecloths on tables designed for 7 or 8 people to sit at, whether you knew them or not. Also, the place was filled with 9 or 10 old men wearing European style caps, sitting at tables or alongside a small bar, smoking cigarettes and drinking beer. It looked like the old taverns in the Polish neighborhoods on the South Side of Chicago, in my Aunt Jane's neighborhood, not far from where I grew up. The old men even dressed and looked like the old men who used to hang out in those taverns in Chicago, and even though they were speaking Czech, it sounded enough like Polish to me to make me feel like I stumbled through a time and space warp.

We stood at the front of the restaurant for a few minutes waiting for someone to pay attention. Finally a waitress came over to us, and when we said "Two for dinner," she smiled and showed us to a table.

It was not a private table, of course, since there was no such thing in this particular restaurant, so we sat across from a younger Czech man wearing the same type of European cap that all the other men wore. The only difference between them and this younger guy was that he had a mustache and a little bit of scruff, and all during the time we sat and talked through our dinner, he looked back and forth at us very suspiciously, like he was trying to decide if we were part of a rival mob gang. Plus, while he was doing this he never said a word to either one of us. Since this place looked just like the kind of mob hangouts you always see on TV or in the movies, I tried to make sure to look friendly and non threatening in any way.

We ordered dinner, but I don't remember how we were able to figure out what was on the menu, since it was all written in Czech. I'm sure Yo was able to figure out most of it, and the waitress seemed to understand a little English. As it turned out, we really had a great meal. I think I had some sort of pot roast or sausage, but whatever it was, it was one of those home cooked type meals from one of those "Old World" type recipes that was incredibly good.

When we were almost done, Yo finally made the first move and said something to the guy across from us. I think she tried German first, since that was a language she knew and many Czech people also know (or so she told me later). Amazingly enough, instead of reaching for his gun, he actually smiled and said something back to her. I wouldn't say he got particularly friendly, but he seemed to understand a few words and asked Yo where we were from. When she told him she was from Holland and I was from America, he gave me that look that seemed to say, "What the hell are you doing here in a place like this?" But I just smiled and probably said something stupid that he wouldn't understand anyway, and by then we were ready to pay our bill and go.

We got back to the train station around 8:30 or so and waited for the shuttle train to arrive. When it finally arrived just before dark, we got in and sat through the short ride to the main train station where we would transfer onto the train to Prague. I put our backpack with our camera and some souvenir postcards and a few other odds and ends in the luggage rack over the seats. We got to the main station and waited on a bench for the Prague train to arrive around 9:00 p.m. When it arrived just after dusk we got on and waited for it to pull out.

While we were waiting we talked about the restaurant, the silver mine, the church made out of human bones and all the other things we had seen during the day. It seemed like it was taking forever for the train to pull out of the station, but in reality it was probably only about 5 minutes, and we were just eager to get back to our hotel.

Suddenly I realized that we did not have our back pack with us! I assumed that I must have left it on the platform bench and told Yo, "I forgot the back pack!" I got up to run off the train and get it before we left, but just as I started getting out of my seat, we could hear the train's horn beeping in two long blasts to signal that it was about to leave.

"It's starting to go!" Yo told me. "I know! I have to get to the bench!" I told her and pushed out into the aisle. Yo was in front of me and we both ran to the train door. As she opened the door, the train started to barely begin pulling out of the station. I wanted to jump out but she was standing in the doorway, trying to decide if she was going to move to let me out.

"You have to hurry!" she said as she finally moved out of the way. "No shit!" I said, or at least I think I said, as I jumped off the train onto the platform. As soon as I made my jump I realized something. That goddamn train was starting to pick up speed **really fast**! I mean it wasn't like in the old movies where it took about 2 or 3 minutes before the train really got rolling. This thing was starting to whiz after just a few seconds. If I didn't pick up the back pack and get back on the train in the next 10 or 12 seconds I wasn't going to make it!

I spotted the bench, ran to it in about 5 seconds flat and had just enough time to pick up the back pack and run back to jump on the train. There was just one problem—**the backpack wasn't there!** I spent about 2 seconds trying to figure out where the back pack could be and then I heard Yo yell "Hurry!"

I looked up and the train was really moving now and Yo was standing on the train step waiting for me to run and jump back on. She was almost even with me already, but I calculated the time it would take me to run the 15 feet from the bench to the edge of the platform and decided I could do it.

I put it into high gear, running as fast as I could for 4 or 5 seconds and was ready to make the leap onto the train step where Yo was standing about 5 feet away from me now, when I hear someone screaming, *"No! No! No! No! NOOOOO!"*

I stopped for a second to look down the train platform to see who was screaming. It was a Czech woman who worked for the railroad and was wearing the railroad company's uniform with a red hat! A second later I looked back at the train just in time to see Yo whizzing by me, standing on the train step. I stood there for a few seconds and watched the whole train go by, speeding along at what I would guess to be 40 or 50 miles per hour already. Whatever speed it was, I knew that it was just way too fast to try to jump on at this point.

Then all of a sudden, it hit me. ***HOLY SHIT ! I'M ALL ALONE IN A COUNTRY WHERE THEY DON'T SPEAK ENGLISH AND I DON'T SPEAK CZECH AND I HAVE TO FIGURE OUT HOW TO GET BACK TO A HOTEL WHICH IS OVER 60 MILES AWAY!***

It was one of those rare times in my life when I was completely stumped as to what to do next. All I could do was stand there, staring at the train as it grew smaller and smaller in the distance and think, "God almighty! What the hell am I going to do?"

After a minute or two I was finally able to put some logical thoughts together. I knew I had enough money on me to buy another train ticket. This was a train station, so there must be more trains coming through here eventually to get back to Prague. I mean this was the 21st century after all. It wasn't like my wagon train broke down in the middle of the desert. So after a couple of minutes, I pulled myself together and started walking towards the end of the platform to find *that goddamn train lady*!

She had gone back inside the station house that she had apparently come out of before she started screaming at me. I didn't really care of she understood English or not at that point. She was the one who got me stuck here, and by God, she was going to help me get out, whether she wanted to or not.

As I soon found out, she didn't really want to help me at all. When I walked into the station house I asked her, "How can I get to Prague?" She acted like she didn't hear me and started walking away, like she was totally pissed off at me for trying to jump back on the train." Oh, no you don't, sweetheart," I thought to my-self and planted myself right in front of her.

"How do I get to Prague?" I repeated. This time she turned around and walked back to a desk to get a piece of paper and started to write something down on it. She still hadn't said a word to me, so I couldn't tell if she understood English or not, so I asked her again, "How do I get to Prague?" She finally looked at me and said, "Calling."

"Calling?" I repeated to her. She nodded her head yes and said "Calling! Calling!" I suppose I must have looked at her like I didn't have the slightest idea about what she was trying to tell me, since I didn't, and then she showed me the paper she had written on. She held up a small piece of paper with KOLIN written on it and said "Calling! Calling!" I had looked at a map of Prague earlier that day and noticed a town called Kolin not too far from Prague. This had to be what she was saying to me! She was giving me the name of the town I had to go to in order to get the next train to Prague, and even though I thought she was saying "Calling," that had to be the Czech pronunciation for Kolin!

"Calling (Kolin)?" I asked her. "That's where I get the next train to Prague?" She nodded her head and closed her eyes like she was saying "Just get the hell out of here, buddy—and don't jump on any more of my trains!" I told her thanks—even though I was sure I could've made the jump back onto the train if she hadn't started her screaming at me—and walked through the tunnel under the tracks to get to the ticket station on the opposite side of the tracks.

I walked to the ticket window and told the clerk I had to get to Prague. The clerk understood enough English to tell me to go to Kolin (he called it "Calling" too) and change trains there. I bought my ticket and waited at the platform he told me to go to. Fortunately, the railroad people seemed to understand enough English so that they could tell me how to get back to Prague.

I got on the train to Kolin and watched the electronic message board that told you what the next stop was. It was actually pretty easy. The stops were about 5 to 10 minutes apart, so you always got plenty of warning before you got to the one you needed. When I finally got to Kolin, I went to the platform number listed on my ticket and the train for Prague arrived right on time. Anytime I wasn't sure if I was in the right place, I asked one of the railroad people and they all understood me pretty well and were all very helpful.

While I was riding on the train to the main station in Prague, I started to wonder if Yo would be waiting for me when I got off. Since I had all the money, I didn't think there was any way she would try to take a train or a taxi back to Kutna Hora, but then I started to wonder if she would be waiting at all. Maybe she would just take the subway and bus back to the hotel, and assume that she had trained me well enough during our previous two days of sightseeing in and around Prague, so that I would know how to do the same thing. Hmmmm… I tried to assume that everything would work out alright, but because I was a total foreigner in a country where I couldn't speak the language, I couldn't help but be a little concerned. I mean, if she wasn't at the train station when I got off, I couldn't call back to the hotel to see if she was there. My cell phone didn't work in Europe and besides I didn't know the name of the hotel where we were staying anyway. And I didn't even know if you could dial information in the Czech Republic, or how you would do it if you could, or even if they would understand me if I did. And what if she wasn't at the train station *or* the hotel? How the hell do you go about asking the police to put out a missing person report if you don't speak their language? And how would I get back to Holland if I didn't leave with the tour bus that was leaving from the hotel the very next morning? I started saying some silent prayers and crossing my fingers and toes and anything else I could cross as the train slowly headed into Prague.

When we got to the station in Prague I felt like something was definitely wrong. It didn't look like the same train station Yo and I had left from that morning. And Yo wasn't there, so either she went on to the hotel or she was waiting for me at a different station. Damn, I wished we both had cell phones right then so I could find out where the hell she was!

After a few minutes of walking around the station, I was sure that this was absolutely a different station than the one we departed from that morning. I walked outside and nothing looked familiar there either. By this time it was well after 11:00 p.m. and there were some people standing on the sidewalk, waiting for buses or someone else. I felt really stupid, but since I didn't know what else to do, I walked up to a woman standing against the building and asked her, "Is this the main train station for Prague?" After being spoiled by the railroad employees who seemed to understand all my questions, I was a little disappointed when she just smiled and shrugged her shoulders. "Do you speak English?" I asked. Again she just smiled and shook her head.

"Crap!" I thought! This is a waste of time! Someone in the train station must be able to tell me where I am! As I walked back into the train station I saw a group of passengers just getting off a train. As I walked by the group, I heard two voices speaking English! Americans! I turned around and saw two young guys in their early twenties wearing back packs and talking together as they walked through the station. "Excuse me!" I said. "Are you guys Americans?"

"Yep," they answered.

"Do you know if this is the main train station for Prague?"

"I sure hope so," the first one said. "If not, I don't know where we are!"

"Great!" I thought. "The only two guys in this whole friggin place that speak English and they're even dumber than me!" But instead of saying that, I just thanked them and walked back to the train platform where I had just gotten off.

It was now almost a half hour since my train got into the station and Yo was still nowhere in sight. I had to assume that she either ended up at a different station than me or got tired of waiting for me and went back to the hotel. I figured that she had to go back to the hotel eventually, no matter what happened, so I decided I would have to put my subway training to the test. I walked out of the station and found the nearest stairway down to the underground. I went to the ticket vending machine and put in the right amount of coins, just like Yo had taught me, and bought my ticket. Then I got on the subway when it came, checked the map in the subway car and remembered which stop I had to get off at. Once I got to my stop, I got off, walked up the steps to the street and waited at the bus stop for the bus that went back to the hotel. I remembered the number of the bus I wanted and got on, paid my fare and made it all the way back to the hotel by myself.

I expected Yo to be waiting for me in the hotel lobby when I walked through the door. *Wrong!* The only people in the lobby when I walked in right before midnight were the night clerk and the night manager. I knew they spoke English, so I walked up to them and asked them if Yo had shown up or left any word for me that she was there or on her way.

"No," they said. They hadn't heard anything from her or seen her all night. "*Shit!* If she's not waiting for me in the room, then I *really* don't know what to do," I thought.

I got to the room and knocked on our door. No answer. I took out my key and opened the door. **_Still no Yo!_** Where could she be? Her train had to get into the station in Prague way earlier than mine, and I spent a good half hour wandering around the station after I arrived before I decided to come back to the hotel. I started pacing back and forth, wondering if I should tell the hotel manager to call the police, file a missing persons report, tell the tour guide I would be staying behind tomorrow to search for my wife, etc., etc., etc. The more I thought about it, the more nervous I got, so I tried to watch TV and calm down. That didn't seem to help much, especially since none of the programs were in English. I tried to decide how long I should wait before hitting the panic button—a half hour, an hour? By that time Russian slave traders could have her bound and gagged in the trunk of a car heading for Moscow!

I waited for about a half hour and stared at the TV while all the bad spy movies from the Cold War era passed before my eyes. I started thinking Yo would end up as a prisoner in a work camp somewhere in Siberia and I would spend the rest of my life wandering around all the train stations in the world yelling "Yo! Yo! Can you hear me?"

Finally, a little after 12:30 I heard a knock on the door! I opened it and ***there she was!*** Of course, the first words out of her mouth were *"Did you take a cab?"* with just a touch of irritation. After I told her how I waited for her at the station and kept wondering what happened to her, she told me where she had been after she whizzed by me in Kutna Hora.

Yo had assumed that I would be taking the next train to Prague, and like me, she also assumed it would be arriving at the same station as the train she was on. She also realized that since the back pack was not on the train platform after I ran over to get it, that we had to have left it in the luggage rack on the shuttle train. So as soon as she got into the main train station in Prague, she found the police office inside the station and tried to submit a lost luggage report. Even though the police were all Czech, she was able to speak a combination of English and German that they could understand, and she got them to call the shuttle train station in Kutna Hora to find out if the back pack was there. The good news was that the station manager in Kutna Hora immediately confirmed that they had the back pack there, so they would ship it to our hotel and our tour guide would be able to retrieve our camera and other belongings the next time she had a tour coming to Prague. After she finally got the police report completed and spent a half an hour waiting for me to show up, she finally came to the same conclusion that I did and decided to head back to the hotel.

Of course, even though it was slightly traumatic for me while I was wondering where Yo was and how I would ever find her if she didn't show up at the hotel, etc., Yo was never worried about anything for one minute. She figured she had taught me well enough so that I could make it back to the hotel on the subway and bus on my own, and that I had enough money to buy an extra train ticket. One way or another, she figured I would be able to find my way back and meet her at the hotel. Of course, she was right as always. She would always tell me things will always take care of themselves if you let them, and after that night I totally believed it.

But if you're ever tempted to jump off a train in the Czech Republic and see if you can get back on it in time before it leaves, take my advice: ***Don't!***

FIRST PARIS, THEN ITALY

Chapter XVII

After we got back to Holland, we had about 8 days to kill until our next trip, which was to Paris. I was looking forward to the trip, of course, because it meant another trip to a European city I had seen in the movies and on TV, but never thought I would actually be able to go there.

We got on the bus in Oss at the same place we had gotten on to go to London and Prague, and as usual, we were the youngest or almost the youngest people on the bus. After a while I got used to traveling with the ouwetjes, but I never got used to the fact that they didn't speak English to me if there was any way they could possibly avoid it. Yo told me many times that it wasn't anything personal, but that they were from the era before English was taught in the primary grades in Holland. Also, most of them were blue collar people without much higher education, so they would not have learned it after finishing their "high school" grades.

The trip to Paris was actually not very scenic or exciting. We rolled into the city about 9 or 10 hours after we left Holland. The hotel was reasonably nice, just like all the other hotels we stayed at on our trips. The staff was friendly and courteous, too—not at all like the stereotypical arrogant, aloof French that I had heard so much about back in the U.S. Actually, just about everyone I met in Europe was friendly and respectful, if not exactly outgoing. But we had absolutely no problem with the French.

We did our usual routine of telling the bus driver and tour guide that we would be exploring the city on our own, thank you, and nobody seemed to mind. We took buses and subways everywhere we went again, and it was just as easy as it was in London and Prague. The only time I had any trouble at all was keeping up with Yo, who had a tendency to read a subway schedule sign or bus sign and rush off in the direction of the next connection without bothering to tell me where she was going, or how soon we had to be there, etc. For whatever reason, she didn't see any reason to let me know where we were going, she just expected me to follow her—which was fine, except that she always moved at twice the speed I was comfortable walking in. On top of that she was a lot smaller than me and could squeeze in between people in crowds without too much trouble, so in no time at all we would get separated. This got to be more than a little aggravating to me, and we had a few terse discussions about it. But I have to say, in all the traveling we did together, this was almost the only thing we ever really argued about. And even that was pretty minor.

Paris was really pretty cool, I have to admit. For all the talk you hear about the French being snobby and rude to Americans, I never saw that once during the time we were there. Granted, it was only for three days and we were dealing with people in the hospitality business for the most part, but still I was a little surprised to see that they really didn't show any animosity towards Americans at all that I could see. And even though I was traveling with a group of Dutch people, I'm sure almost everyone knew I was an American. It's hard to hide it when you don't speak any language other than English and you do that with an American accent!

We did a whirlwind tour by bus and subway and saw the Eiffel Tower, the Arc D'Triumph, the Louvre and the Cathedral of Notre Dame. They were all lots of fun and very interesting to see, but I think I liked seeing the gargoyles on the roof of the Cathedral of Notre Dame the best. We had to wait in line for about an hour, and climb up about 150 steps to get up to the roof, but once we were up there you could see all the weird and bizarre sculptures that looked like demons looking down on the city. You don't see stuff like that outside of a theme park in the U.S., so I was pretty impressed to think that these were sculptures created back in the 1100s or 1200s. (I was never very good at keeping track of the dates that things were built or painted. Yo always knew when something was made and kept telling me when it originated, but I could never remember. All I knew was that it was well over 800 or 900 years old, and for someone coming from a country that thinks buildings built in the 1950s are ancient, that was *old*!)

The only time I didn't appreciate Paris was when we had to take the bus back to our hotel one night. We had taken the subway to the main bus station for the bus that would get us back, and it was pretty late on a Sunday night, around 10:00 or 11:00 p.m.

There is a large population of North Africans in Paris from Morocco, Algeria, and Tunisia who come there because they work cheap and there are a lot of low paying jobs available for them selling souvenirs to tourists, as well as other jobs. Apparently, a lot of them were going home that night after a long day of trying to sell trinkets outside the Louvre, the Eiffel Tower and other tourist spots. Unfortunately, they all seemed to be taking the same bus as Yo and me. Once we got on the bus, so many people got on with us we were literally so jammed inside the bus that you couldn't move.

As I was smashed between two of the Africans, I started to wonder if either Yo or I would be able to raise our arms to pull the signal cord when we got to our stop. For about 3 or 4 miles, all I could do was stand there with my arms pinned to my sides, looking at Yo, who seemed to be enjoying my discomfort immensely. Even though she was giggling and having a great time watching me, I was definitely not happy about nearly being squashed to death on a bus. It was actually one of the only times I was really aggravated during any of our trips, and I looked at Yo and said "We are **never** doing this again!" Even though I was really pissed off, she still thought it was all very funny.

After a few miles, the majority of the Africans had gotten off, and I was starting to calm down. Eventually I was able to see the humor in the whole situation. When we finally got off the bus, I told Yo that after getting so close and personal with the North Africans on the bus, I thought I might be an honorary member of their tribe!

We got back from Paris on June 5th and three days later we were on our way to Italy! This was one of the longest trips we took and one of the more fun trips for me personally, because we actually met Dutch people who would *talk to me ! In English!*

The trip to Italy by bus required an overnight stay in Germany, and even that turned out to be fun. We stopped in some out of the way town near the Swiss border and checked into the hotel we had all been assigned to. This one was a little on the old fashioned side, more like two or three large houses all joined together with rooms on different levels for all the ouwetjes on the trip.

Amazingly enough, there were some couples on the trip who were closer to our age than usual, too. One of them turned out to be very friendly and we ended up spending a lot of time with them and two men who were traveling together but weren't gay. They were both married, but they had wives that didn't like to travel for some reason. Bram was in his seventies, and Johann was in his late fifties or early sixties.

I would have thought this was a bit of a strange arrangement except for the fact that I knew Yo's dad traveled to many countries around the world the same way. Her mom did not like traveling at all and her dad was just the opposite, so every year he would go to South Africa or Indonesia or the U.S. or any other place he wanted to visit with a friend of his, and no one seemed to find anything strange about this at all. The best part about all these people was that they didn't seem to mind conversing in English and for once I could understand what people were saying when we ate together at a restaurant!

We had dinner at the restaurant next to the hotel and some of the Dutch people apparently had never eaten spaetzel before. I knew all about it and had eaten it many times at my ex in-laws house when I was married to my first wife, Karen. That was one of my ex-mother-in-law's specialties, and I actually thought it was pretty good. The Dutch people that were sitting next to me at the restaurant apparently didn't like the looks of it though, because one of them said, "I guess we have to say goodbye to good Dutch food for the next 10 days!" "Wow," I thought, "that's a switch! They're actually serving something in a European restaurant that I like eating and the Dutch don't particularly care for!"

After dinner we decided to walk around the town, what little there was of it. I don't know what the name of the town was, but it was basically about 15 or 20 homes all grouped together around the hotel and restaurant, with almost nothing else around it but corn fields.—kind of an Old World type Iowa town. Yo and I walked up and down a few of the streets and turned into one where there was a group of people sitting in the front yard, and we recognized two of them from our bus. One of the women in the group yelled out "Nederlander?" to us, asking if we were Dutch, and Yo yelled back "Nederlander and American!" The woman then said something in Dutch and waved us in, obviously asking us to join the party.

It turned out that the group was celebrating this woman's birthday and they were inviting anyone who came walking by to join their party. Yo could talk to them easily since she spoke fluent German. I didn't get to talk much, since they also didn't seem to want to say much in English, but I got a couple of glasses of wine out of the deal, so it turned out good after all.

After a half hour or so, we went back to the hotel. We had a little bit of comedy when we ran into Bram, the older half of the male couple on our bus, who seemed to be lost. His room was on a different floor of the hotel than everyone else's and he was having trouble figuring out where it was. I have to admit, it wasn't an easy one to find, because you had to go down a stairwell and go through a long corridor to get there. But eventually we were able to find it and get him into his room. He thought it was pretty funny, too. So we had met some people that didn't mind speaking English, we got ourselves invited to some German lady's birthday party and the next day we would be going through Switzerland and into Italy. On to the next adventure!

THE EMBASSY GAME—PART TWO

Chapter XVIII

I taly was a lot of fun. We went to Florence, Pisa, Sienna and Rome. We saw the Leaning Tower of Pisa, the Vatican, the Coliseum and the ruins of the Forum. We even had our picture taken at the Trevi Fountain. All in all, we had a great trip, and like I said, the thing that made it even more enjoyable for me was the fact that there were people there I could actually talk to besides Yolande. Peter and Karin were the couple about my age and we usually sat with them and Bram and Yohan during our breakfast and dinner meals. We got to know them pretty well and took down email messages to keep in touch after the trip was over (Of course we never did, except to get pictures emailed to us from Karin after we unexplainably "lost" at least a dozen pictures we had taken on our digital camera in Rome.)

When we got back to Yolande's parent's house after the trip to Italy, we found a package waiting for us. Before we had left on our trip to Paris, we had called Cyn back in Long Beach to let her know the latest requirement from the U.S. Embassy to allow us to petition to have Yo's visa reinstated. During one of the periods between our trips—I think it was after we got back from Prague—we received the _certified_ copies of my divorce decrees from my daughter. Now we could go back to the embassy and finally submit the paperwork that was needed to get the ball rolling to bring Yo back to America.

Wrong! After we got to the embassy, waited over a half hour to get inside, and stood in line for another half hour inside, we walked up to window #5 once more to come face to face with—***Vivian Wyatt! Again!***

This time I was ready for her—or so I thought. She remembered me.

"Oh, Mr. Durack, I'm glad to see you are back. You now have the paperwork required to submit your application?" she asked.

"Yep. It's all here. Certified copies of my divorce decrees and all."

"Very good," Vivian said. "And now where are the copies of your last three years' tax returns?"

"Huh?"

"You know that you still must provide copies of your last three years tax returns, do you not?"

"No, nobody told me about that when I was here the last time."

"Yes, but Mr. Durack, if you had read the requirements as they are posted on the internet website, you would have known this. I am afraid I cannot take your application until we receive these documents."

I couldn't believe it! Now we had to call home for _another_ set of documents to give to the embassy before we could submit Yo's application! The only good thing about it was that I had at least another 6 weeks before I was scheduled to go home!

I had called Cyn and told her our predicament. We needed to have her go into the room which Yo and I had been renting from her and pick up the tax return files in a drawer underneath my computer table. I told her exactly where it was and the years we needed to have sent to us. She told us she would try to get to it within the next _week_—a little longer than I wanted to hear, but I knew she was extremely busy and going through some major financial problems with her business. Besides, we really had no choice except to wait.

So I was extremely pleased when we returned from Italy to find a package waiting for us from Cyn's address. This could only be the copies of the tax returns we had sent for.

I opened the box and couldn't believe my eyes.

Instead of sending my personal tax returns for the previous three years, Cyn had sent copies of my *partnership* returns from an independent business I was involved in. The files even had labels on the front that read _**"Holland Durack Productions"**_! How could *ANYBODY* think these were my personal tax returns I wondered?

For a couple of seconds I was tempted to throw the box across the room, but I was somehow able to resist. "What's wrong?" Yo asked me as she and her mom watched me struggle to keep from screaming.

"They sent the **_wrong returns_**!" I yelled.

They looked at me for a few seconds, trying to understand.

"How could they do that?" Yo asked.

"Exactly!" I shouted. "How the hell could ***ANYBODY*** do that?"

It took a few minutes, but I was finally able to calm down enough to explain to Yo and Rieke what had happened. I couldn't believe that after I had told Cyn how important it was for us to get the returns to enable Yo to submit her application, and how carefully and precisely I had told her where to find them, that they still sent the wrong returns. And they were even marked as the "*Holland Durack Productions*" partnership returns! I could not understand how anybody could make such a mistake! And now it was going to cost us a lot more time!

I sat and seethed for about a half hour and then sent Cyn an email advising her of the mistake. I again told her that I needed the documents ASAP in the hope that it would not take her another week to either look for the returns or delegate someone else to do it. We exchanged a few terse emails back and forth, and I later found out that the couple who had moved into our room while I was gone had taken it upon themselves to move my files into the garage in Long Beach, thus explaining why it was so difficult to track the needed returns down. But in the final analysis, it didn't really matter.

Now I knew it was going to take a lot longer than 12 weeks to process Yo's application. I had already been in Europe nearly 8 weeks and now we had to wait for the *right* tax returns to get sent to us. Since we were already scheduled to leave on our next trip to Ireland in 5 days, we knew we wouldn't get the returns any earlier than when we returned from Ireland 10 days later.

We decided to finish the trips we had already scheduled for Ireland and Belgium and keep our fingers crossed that the tax returns we needed would arrive before my 12 week time limit was up.

YANKEE, COME HOME

Chapter XIX

We left on our trip for Ireland on June 22nd. It felt great to be going back to my parents' homeland, a place where I had tons of cousins and relatives, but had only been to once when I was seven years old. I thought about how it would be interesting to see how much I would remember about a place I had been to 47 years ago and how much it must have changed since then.

I wasn't disappointed. Ireland was now a modern country, supposedly having the best economy in Europe, thanks to the internet and computer related multinational companies that set up their headquarters there in the late 1990s. It definitely was no longer the slightly backward country that I remembered from my previous visit 47 years ago, but the countryside was still fresh and green and beautiful, and the people were still friendly and sociable. Best of all, the way of life still seemed a lot calmer and unhurried than the U.S. Of course, this was probably mostly due to the fact that we were with a group of tourists from Holland who were all mostly retirees and we were all mostly calm and relaxed ourselves. I'm sure that in the hustle and the bustle of the cities, it's just as frantic a rat race as it is in London, Chicago or New York. But the 10 day bus tour we took through the rolling hills and countryside of Galway, the Burren, Blarney Castle and a number of other places where the biggest traffic jams were caused by herds of sheep on the road made everything else seem to fade away.

Yo particularly seemed to like the countryside and people we met during our trip. So much so, that she surprisingly told me halfway through it that she wouldn't mind living in Ireland for a few years. I thought she was kidding at first, just trying to make me feel good because this was one of the few places in Europe where I would have no language barrier at all, and the country that I knew the most about besides the United States and could relate to almost as well. But she was actually serious about exploring the possibility of working and living there.

The more I thought about it, the more I actually liked the idea. After all, I already had an Irish passport because I had taken advantage or Ireland's dual citizenship offer—(if your parents or grandparents were born in Ireland, you could also become a citizen)—and I always thought it would be fun to go back to my roots for a while. On top of that, the way things were going, we didn't know how long it might take to get Yo's visa reinstated to allow her to come back to the U.S., and we were both getting pretty tired of the bureaucracy and hypocrisy of the U.S. government.

Here I was, thousands of miles from my home, waiting for my documents to prove I could support my wife,—who was supporting herself for at least twenty years before I even met her—and we were both in Europe because she had been exiled from the U.S. for the heinous crime of not leaving the country when she was supposed to!

Now, I understand why some people feel that this is exactly what we should have had to do. The United States has laws and people who don't obey those laws have to face the consequences. Fine. In most cases, I actually do agree with that. I can even understand why Yo's deportation was officially necessary. You can't have one set of rules for people from one country and another set of rules for people from another country. My argument is with the severity and bureaucratic awkwardness of the entire system.

Look at it this way: Yo was in the United States for over 11 years and nobody ever seemed to mind. She did not use any of our "free" medical facilities, educational facilities or any other government supplied facilities that people are so worried about illegal immigrants misusing or abusing. She worked only at jobs that paid cash so she did not have to pay any taxes, it's true, but neither would anyone else who took those jobs because the payments were never reported to anyone.

She caused no crimes and actually made many friends among the people she worked with and that knew her from the murder mystery shows she helped stage and costume. As far as her taking away jobs from American workers is concerned, the jobs she took were jobs that would not support anyone else. She was able to support herself with them only because of the barter arrangement she had with Cyn for free room and board. On the other hand, she did contribute to the economy on a very limited basis by buying clothes from thrift shops, food and supplies from local restaurants and stores and general purchases, small as they might be. All in all, I think it's realistic to say that she ended up contributing much more to the economy than she took out. And because she did not obey the law that says you can only stay here for so long if you are from somewhere else, she was exiled for an indefinite time period that could possibly take up to ten years.

Now, let's say for the moment that even if it might be unfair, that's the law and she knew what the consequences would be if she were caught. Yes, that's true. And, if that's the law, then she and I had no choice but to accept the consequences and have her return to Holland. But why should it ever take nearly seven weeks of sitting in a prison in El Paso, Texas for that to be taken care of? The unofficial estimate of the cost of keeping a detainee in the El Paso detention center is over $100 per day. Assuming that's correct, (and it seems reasonable that it would be at least that much, if not more), the cost to keep Yo in the detention center for 6 weeks and 5 days was over $4700. On top of that, the day she was released to be sent back to Holland, two U.S. Customs Service personnel had to accompany her on the flight from El Paso to Atlanta and stay at the Atlanta airport after she boarded the plane to Amsterdam to make sure she didn't get off before it departed! Assuming that the detention center guards assigned to accompany Yo on the flight to Atlanta made around $12.00 per hour, this would result in an extra cost of over $ 400 with fringe benefits being taken into consideration. Plus there is also the cost of the flights from El Paso to Atlanta for Yo and her traveling companions and Yo's flight from Atlanta to Amsterdam. A very conservative estimate would put this at anywhere from $1000 to $1500.

Now I admit, this is not a very scientific cost study, since all of the costs are being estimated, but I think it's fair to say that the entire process of having Yo deported for the crime of staying in America longer than she was legally allowed to cost the U.S. taxpayers well over $6,000! And this is definitely a *rock bottom minimum*, when you consider that most of the other detainees that Yo was incarcerated with spent far longer than 7 weeks in detention, with the average time frame being anywhere between 3 and 6 months, and in some cases some well over *a year* for detainees who were also political exiles from their own countries, you can see how expensive the inefficiency of this system has become.

Wouldn't it make more sense, financially and ethically, to give someone who is arrested for overstaying their visa in the U.S. the option of paying a *fine* and paying any back state or federal taxes due on their earnings or estimated earnings in order to continue living here instead of treating them like criminals and incurring costs of *over $6,000 at a minimum* to have them shipped back to their home countries? If they couldn't pay the back taxes and fines or *wouldn't* pay them for any reason, then I agree, they would have to be deported as expeditiously as possible. But if they are <u>willing</u> to bite the bullet and pay their fines and/or taxes, *as millions of American citizens do every year for other "victimless" crimes, such as tax evasion and traffic violations,* shouldn't they at least be given the chance to continue working in and contributing to the U.S. economy and society?

Again, I'm not talking about people who overstay their visas and commit a crime, or come into this country without any visa and commit crimes, or who plot against the U.S. with a terrorist group, or anyone who does anything even *remotely* illegal other than their immigration violation. I agree that those people should be incarcerated, put on trial and treated as the criminals they are, in addition to being shipped out of the U.S. on a permanent basis. But for the people whose only "crime" is trying to find a better way of life for themselves or their families, or those who actually contribute something to our society and/or economy in some way, no matter how small, and who can pay for their non-compliance with our immigration laws, as outlined above—why can't we be reasonable enough and economically practical enough to recognize that ***<u>it is more beneficial to our country to keep these people here instead of sending them away?</u>***

I know a lot of people in the U.S. still find this unacceptable on any grounds. They argue that if we start to make exceptions to our immigration laws we will only encourage more violations of an already eroded principle of U.S. government. I understand their concerns, but again, I have to say that regardless of how long a principle has been in place or what its original purpose was, you still have to ask yourself, ***<u>Does it still make sense?</u>***

In other words, no matter what it did or didn't accomplish in the past, does keeping it in place now do more good than harm? From *my* perspective, paying over $ 6,000 per person for anyone caught staying in this country longer than they were supposed to, who spend more money into the economy than they take out, or provide a service or benefit to American society that would not otherwise be provided *__just doesn't make sense!__* There are _other_ ways of dealing with this problem, which would end up as a win/win scenario and from a practical standpoint, would contribute more money to the economy than it would cost. But I'm sure the opponents of any leniency in U.S. immigration policy will continue to stand by their dogma of absolutely no change at any cost, no exceptions, no mitigating circumstances, and most of all, *__no mercy!__*

I know there are some people who read this who will never agree with me, and I know they have a right to their opinion too. I would never try to force anyone to agree with me, but instead would hope to persuade them with logic and common sense. But I have to say, the atmosphere of narrow minded intolerance that seems to be dividing many Americans on immigration was starting to get to me, and the idea of living in Ireland in the near future or somewhere with a more tolerant viewpoint on this subject suddenly appealed to me more than it had in the past. We talked to a lot of the people we met at the hotels and restaurants to find out how difficult it might be to find work in Ireland, where the best places to live might be, the relative expensiveness of various areas, etc., etc.

As we headed back to Holland, Yo and I both decided that if things didn't change for the better soon, that this was a possibility that we were seriously going to explore.

ALONE AGAIN, NATURALLY

Chapter XX

Shortly after we returned from Ireland we finally received the ***holy grail***—the missing tax returns that we needed to go to the embassy one more time and apply for the re-instatement of Yo's visa! We still had one more trip planned, however—a short three day trip to Belgium, so we decided to put off a visit to the embassy again until that was out of the way.

The trip to Belgium was pleasant enough, but after seeing England, Ireland, Paris, Italy and Prague, I was a little bit spoiled. Belgium was just a little bit too much like Holland as far as I was concerned, and although it definitely wasn't *un*pleasant, there wasn't anything all that different about it that we hadn't seen somewhere else. So we ate at the restaurants, took pictures of the town squares and took the canal boat rides. But after we got back to Uden, we knew the time was coming when I would have to return to the U.S. and earn some more money. My cash reserve was pretty well depleted by this time and it was now extremely obvious that the whole process would take <u>*much*</u> longer than 12 weeks to resolve. How much longer, we didn't know, but it was time to take the application forms along with *all* the necessary documents back to the embassy and find out.

The week after we returned from Belgium, we made the trip into Amsterdam one more time, to submit the application forms along with the tax returns. Amazingly enough, this time they accepted everything! However, not before the clerk at the window we went to gave Yolande a stern lecture about overstaying her visa to the U.S. and making her promise never to do it again—like we ever wanted to go through this bureaucratic nightmare again! But after a half an hour we were out of the embassy and the only thing we still had left to do was for Yo to get her physical from an embassy-approved doctor to make sure she didn't have any communicable diseases to spread around in the U.S.

It seemed almost surreal that the paperwork ordeal was almost over, but we still weren't out of the woods yet. Once Yo got her physical, she would have to go back to the embassy at least one more time to have an in-depth interview with an embassy official who would then make a recommendation about whether or not she could return to the U.S. So we still didn't know how long it would take to resolve! The estimates were anywhere from 3 months to a year or longer. We both realized now that I would have to go back to America and wait for her. I didn't have enough money to stay in Europe without a job any longer, and I didn't have time to try to learn Dutch or any other language and get a job over there. I needed money! It was time for me to go back.

The week before I was to leave for America, we went to house sit at Yo's sister's house in Maastricht, a city on the border between Holland and Belgium for three days. Our sole duties were to pick up the mail and water the plants while her sister was at some kind of convention with her kids. During that time, we had to go to the main library in town to use the internet so I could book my plane tickets. I spent a couple of hours trying to find the best deals, and eventually booked a flight back to San Diego, with a week's stop over in Chicago so I could visit friends and relatives there and in Wisconsin. I figured it might be a while before I got back that way again, and it would be good to see my daughter, Marilyn, who lived in Appleton, along with some of my old friends in Chicago.

After I was able to make the flight arrangements, I sent an email to Cyn, advising her of when I would be returning. To my everlasting amazement, she sent me a reply that stated, among other things, that she would be leaving for a trip to Australia about a month after I returned, and I would have to sleep in the family room until then because "Michael and Melissa would still be in my old room *because she was pregnant now*!"

I was absolutely stunned! I knew that Cyn was going to be renting out our room while Yo and I were in Europe, and I certainly didn't blame her for that, but I had been told it would be just to provide a little "get away" for her friends, Michael and Melissa, while we were gone. Apparently, there was some problem with the living arrangements they had with one of their relatives, and it would work out very nicely for them to be able to move out for a few months. That was all fine with me. But I never expected not to have a room to return to when I came back!

I sent Cyn a second email politely inquiring as to how long Michael and Melissa would be staying in the room after I returned. I was hoping to get a reply that said they would be leaving within a few days after I got back so that I could have my room and my own bed back. Instead, I received another cryptic message that said we would work everything out when we "both" got back. Hmmmm…

Not knowing what to think, I sent out several emails to friends and acquaintances asking if they had a spare room available for rent. Trying to find an apartment on my own was out of the question, since I didn't have a job and had been self employed (actually more like partially unemployed) for the last 10 months. I even sent an email to Amanda asking her if it would be possible to stay with her in her apartment in Oceanside for a while—although I'm sure neither one of us actually looked forward to that type of arrangement. I mean how many single young women would want their father sleeping on the couch in their apartment every night? However, Mandy put on her best game face and said that would be fine if I needed a place to stay. I decided to wait and see what happened when I returned to Long Beach before making any further decisions.

I talked to Yo about Cyn's apparent indifference to my dilemma. As always, she was downright unemotional about it, saying that there was probably too much going on in Cyn's life for her to think the whole thing through clearly, and that once I got back we would figure out what to do. I always admired Yo for her ability to see the practical side of almost any problem and think everything through calmly and unemotionally, but this was one time I wished she was a little less neutral. I mean, I could understand why Cyn wanted paying renters in the room while we were gone, but I thought if it was me, I would *NEVER* tell someone that they couldn't have their room back when they returned from a trip, unless there was a damn good reason. And I didn't see what Melissa getting pregnant had to do with my not being able to come back to the room I thought was mine to rent as long as I wanted. Unfortunately, there was nothing I could do about it except wait and seethe.

Two days before my return flight from Amsterdam we took the train to Utrecht to stay with Yo's brother and wife, Bart and Dees (although in Holland, a lot of people don't see the need to have a marriage ceremony, so technically she was not a "wife," but for all practical purposes, they were a husband and wife with two kids.) Utrecht was a lot closer to Amsterdam than Uden, so it would be easier for me to take the train to the airport from there instead of from Uden.

There was a heat wave in Holland the week before I left, with temperatures in the 90s for most of the week. One of the bad things I learned about Yo's relatives and Dutch people in general is they don't seem to mind the heat much. I was absolutely broiling for almost five days inside Yo's parents' house and later at Bart and Dees' house, but for some reason they didn't feel a need to open any windows or use any house fans! I couldn't believe I was the only one sitting inside and sweating all day long, but everyone else acted like there wasn't any problem.

I assumed that Yo's parents didn't have any fans because Yo had always told me that Dutch people were notoriously cheap and didn't buy anything unless they really needed it, and I figured a heat wave that only lasted 6 or 7 days a year probably didn't qualify as anything drastic enough to require the purchase of a fan! But to my amazement, there were no fans set up at Bart and Dees' house either, although they did try to crack the sliding glass door and catch a breeze to cool off the house. These Dutch people must have a much higher tolerance for warm temperatures than I do, I thought.

I did my best to try not to complain. I figured if the Dutch could stand it, I should be able to stand it too. But I was actually glad in one way to be leaving Holland on July 19th—to escape the heat! (I later found out that Yo's parents actually *did* have house fans in their house the whole time that I was there. They just didn't see any need to use them during the ungodly heat wave! I mean, **jeez**! Sometimes I just said to myself, "What is **wrong** with these people?")

Despite the heat, of course, I didn't want to leave Yo. I have to admit I was a little nervous about leaving her and not knowing how long it would be before I saw her again. I could only hope that the embassy would be lenient on her, realize that she hadn't done any harm to anyone by overstaying her visa, and grant her a new one as soon as possible. She rode the train to the airport with me the morning

I had to leave. (Another curious thing about the Dutch: when anyone in my family went off on a trip to another country, we always had an entourage of family and well wishers who went along with us to send us off at the airport. The Dutch let you do it on your own. They just don't see what the big deal is!)

We had our own private moments for a few minutes before I got on the plane, but it definitely wasn't anything extremely emotional or sentimental. Yo's attitude was, "OK, this sucks, but it's something that we have to do, so I'll see you when I see you!"

As usual, she was absolutely right, just more practical about the whole thing than most people. I gave her a kiss goodbye and got on the plane for Chicago. Once we got up in the air I started wondering about a bunch of things:

How long would it take before Yo got her visa reinstated to come back to the U.S.?

How long would it take me to find a job and make some money?

What would I tell any prospective employers about what I'd been doing for the past ten months?

What should I tell them about where my wife was and when she was coming back?

And perhaps the biggest question of all: *Where was I going to live?*

SOMEONE'S BEEN SLEEPING IN MY BED

Chapter XXI

I arrived in Chicago on the evening of Wednesday, July 20th and John Stice, my best friend from my boyhood picked me up and let me stay at his house in Tinley Park for two nights. I had known John since I was about 5 years old and he was 6, and he has been the best friend I have ever had during my entire lifetime. He used to torment me when I was a kid, just like a big brother usually treats his little brother, but over the years we got into enough fights and other shared experiences to form a lifelong bond.

Out of all the people I know today, John is the one that I would turn to first if I was in trouble and needed help. He has been there for me when I really needed a friend, and it was good to be able to stay with him and his wife, Kathy, who I also knew since high school for a couple of days. On my last night there, John and I joined two of my other best friends, Denny LaFaire and Steve McMillan at the White Sox game. The Sox lost and we all drank way too much beer, but we had a great time.

The next day, I got myself a rental car and drove up to Wisconsin to see my daughter Marilyn in Appleton, and my ex-in laws in Oshkosh. Even though Marilyn's mom and I had been divorced for over 12 years, we were still on good terms and I was also still on good terms with her parents. So I decided it was time to visit the folks and give them the Green Bay Packer nesting dolls we had bought for them in Prague (Prague, of all places!), and the other souvenirs we had bought for Marilyn. We had a nice visit and then it was time to drive down to Milwaukee to fly back to San Diego. From there I would drive back to Long Beach to meet with Cyn, Michael and Melissa and try to find out what the hell the deal was with our room.

I got back to Long Beach on July 24th and immediately changed clothes to go to a job interview in Newport Beach that I had set up on the internet the week before in Holland. I didn't want to waste any time in finding a new job and earning some money because I knew I would have bills to pay—but I hadn't realized how far behind I was in paying some of them.

I found out within a day of returning that the bills which were supposed to be paid in my absence had been ignored for almost two months. It was one of many problems which came up while I was in Europe that I still have a hard time understanding exactly why it had to happen at all. But I could make the minimum payments required and get caught up temporarily without too much trouble. The main thing I wanted to find out was, when would I get my room and my own bed back??

I requested a meeting with Cyn, Michael and Melissa as soon as I got back to get the status of the room straightened out. I foolishly thought that Michael and Melissa might even volunteer to leave, since they knew they were preventing me from getting back into the room with my bed and bedroom furniture, etc., and that I had been living there until they swooped in three months ago.

No such luck. Not only did no one else seem the slightest bit concerned that I had been, in effect, evicted from the room I had been renting and now had to sleep on a couch in the den, Cyn even started the discussion off by announcing that the most important thing for any of us was to make sure Melissa stayed pregnant!

I was again momentarily stunned, wondering why that should be the most important thing in my life right then, but I decided to keep my mouth shut and listen, hoping that some explanation would be following soon. However, there was no other explanation provided other than Michael had already installed a window air conditioner in the bedroom to make sure Melissa and her baby didn't get overheated, and Cyn obviously felt that the mere fact that she was pregnant was reason enough for both of them to stay there.

Now, pissed off as I was, I wasn't about to tell a pregnant woman she had to get out of the room she was living in and find someplace to live, even if they did join forces to evict me simply because it was more convenient than leaving. I wanted to scream, but I decided the best thing to do in the long run was simply to find another place to live. However, until I got a job and had a regular income, I didn't see any realistic way to do that. So I resigned myself to sleeping on the couch in the family room until I could get a job, and set out more determined than ever to make that happen ASAP!

During the course of the next two weeks, I had 4 more job interviews, and amazingly enough, the last one was a winner! I got called back for a second interview and on or about August 14th, I received a call advising I had been hired as a Controller for a fruit processing company and would start on August 21st! I immediately started scouring the local newspapers for apartments to rent, and found one within 3 or 4 days that I thought would be affordable and had the kind of old fashioned, funky layout with hardwood floors that Yo would like. I decided to tell my prospective landlords that Yo was detained in Holland because she had to help take over the "family business" due to a sudden illness in the family. This way I could also tell them that we didn't know exactly how long it would take before she could come back to live in Long Beach with me, but we had high hopes that it would be before the end of the year. Even though my prospective landlady seemed a little skeptical about my story at first, she ultimately decided that I would make an acceptable tenant and rented the apartment to me.

This was the same story I had told the fruit company people when I interviewed for the job, since I didn't want to take a chance that they might get spooked about employing someone in a management position whose wife had been deported from the U.S. Of course, that had nothing to do with whether or not I could do the job, and it really shouldn't have had any influence one way or the other over whether I got the job or not, but when it comes to job interviews you never know. I had been involved in at least two situations in the past where I had later been told that a seemingly innocuous comment I had made during an interview was enough to change the interviewer's mind about whether or not I was the right candidate. I was not about to take a chance at being turned down for a job because of Yolande's immigration problems, so I lied. I hate to admit it, but that was the only way I felt I could be sure that the whole thing wouldn't be used against me to keep me from getting a job.

It seemed to work fine in both cases, although now I had to make sure I remembered to tell the same story to anyone who asked me about Yo's return at my new company or if my landlords ever questioned me about it. Luckily, it didn't come up very often, and when it did, I was able to remember the official story. I know that this was technically lying, but I figured that it really wasn't anybody else's business anyway, and that it really had no bearing on whether or not I was capable of doing my job or paying the rent. Therefore, I rationalized that it wasn't harming anyone and made life a little easier for me. It may not have been the most honest way of dealing with the situation, but under the circumstances, I wasn't willing to take any more chances that might end up delaying Yo's return from Holland. And on top of that, I was determined to get my own apartment so that I didn't have to sleep on the couch in the den anymore!

I signed the lease for our new apartment and told Michael and Melissa that I would be moving out on Sunday, September 3rd, the day before Labor Day. They seemed to be rather pleased at this since they would now have the run of the entire downstairs section of the house all to themselves. I had already told Cyn I was looking for another place to live before I signed the lease, and although she didn't seem particularly happy about the whole turn of events, she did say to me, "Do whatever works out best for you and Yo."

I recruited a couple of friends along with my ex-wife, Karen, her husband John and my daughter Amanda, and we completed the move to my new apartment in Long Beach on what seemed like the hottest day of the year. As soon as I had the furniture arranged, and most of the boxes unpacked I took some digital pictures of the whole apartment and emailed them to Yo to seek her approval. Luckily, she approved.

The worst part about Yo still being in Holland was that I couldn't talk to her on a daily basis. Due to the 8 hour time difference and the fact that she was working different hours each week, each phone call had to be planned, usually on the weekend when I didn't have to be at work.

Yo had found a job in Holland working at a CD factory, and in what seemed to me like another quirk in Dutch culture, her shift changed from 7:00 to 3:30 one week to 3:30 to midnight the next week to midnight to 7:00 the next week. Each week she had a different work schedule, and with the 8 hour time difference between Holland and California, it made it relatively tricky to find a good time to call her. As usual, I thought it was very strange, but she didn't seem to find anything unusual about it! We generally saved our calls until the weekend, when we could spend an hour or more on the phone and sent emails to each other if anything important came up in between.

During this time I became extremely busy with my new job, which was actually very demanding in many ways, and started the all too familiar routine of 12 to 15 hour work days in the corporate world. I kept calling Yo every few days, asking if she had gotten any word from the U.S. embassy about when her interview would take place, and just about every time I asked she said no. After a while she even got annoyed with me for asking so often, so I tried my best not to ask anymore.

Finally, around the beginning of November, Yo called to tell me her interview would take place on Thanksgiving Day! I was ecstatic! Even though she reminded me that no one would give her any estimate of how long it might take her to get her visa restored after that, I had to send emails to everybody I knew telling them that Yo could be coming home as early as year end. I don't know why I thought it would happen that quickly, but I couldn't help getting optimistic. I really thought we might finally be seeing the light at the end of the tunnel!

I had to think that—it was the only way I could keep from losing hope.

EMBASSY GAME FINALS

Chapter XXII

The day after Thanksgiving Yo called to let me know how the interview went. Overall, it sounded like it went fairly well, although I was a little concerned when she told me about some of the questions put to her by the embassy official, such as:

"Ms. Wassenberg, why did you stay in the United States so long after you knew your visa had expired?"

"Well, nobody checked."

Yo was answering with her usual honesty, which in most cases was good, but I'm sure the embassy official was expecting a little more remorse, whether it was genuine or not. Unfortunately, Yo could not bring herself to pretend for anyone, and it sounded to me like her straightforward style was a little unnerving to her interviewer.

"Ms. Wassenberg, if you had the chance to overstay your visa again, would you do it?"

This time there was just a long pause on her part, and the interviewer fortunately had a sense of humor. He finally had to laugh at Yo's attempt to be honest by not answering the question and simply moved on.

The bottom line was that the interview seemed to go well, but now she had to wait to be notified what the next step would be. Eventually her file was supposed to be sent to the Department of Homeland Security office in Frankfurt, Germany! Why Homeland Security had an office in Frankfurt, Germany of course was not explained, nor could anyone tell her how long it might be before she received any further indication of how long the process might take. She, and I, just had to continue to sit and wait until we heard back from someone—the Immigration Department, the U.S. Consul or the Department of Homeland Security. She and I never knew exactly who the actual notifications were supposed to come from, it just all became one giant bureaucratic blur. So Yo, of course, was resigned to the fact that there was nothing further that could be done, while I, of course, felt like I had to try to do something to speed things along.

I had sent emails to the two U.S. Senators from California, Barbara Boxer and Dianne Feinstein, asking for their help. I was hoping that, between the two of them, one of them would be able to wield some clout and help cut through the red tape.

Unfortunately, this was not a big enough issue to get much attention from either one of them. I received two politely worded emails back from their offices explaining that they sympathized with my situation, but they could not and would not do anything that might be construed as interfering with the U.S. Immigration Department's procedures.

Actually, I understood exactly why it had to be that way, but I had been hoping that they might be able to make some type of exception in this case. It took a few weeks before I got the answer from both senators, but in both cases it was basically the same: Sorry, no can do!

During this time my job got slowly more and more demanding. I started out working normal 8 or 9 hour days, reviewing accounting reports, supervising my department and preparing loan requests from our credit lender. But around the beginning of November, things started to change. The company was coming up to the fiscal year end reporting period and we desperately needed to hire two people in the Accounting department. For some strange reason, the Human Resources department had a difficult time in obtaining candidates for these positions, so my boss told me to hire the first two people who interviewed for the open jobs—which I did. One of them was able to work independently without much supervision, but the other person was a disaster.

All of this training and fixing of major mistakes made by this new employee, combined with the increasing demands from our corporate office soon began to take its toll, especially on my boss. He was really a great boss to work for, technically smart with a sense of humor and compassion for the employees who worked under him—a rare combination in the world of corporate accounting! However, unbeknownst to me, he had been working incredibly long hours for months before I ever started on the job, trying to cover far more duties than any one person could ever do. He usually stated his workday around 5:00 or 6:00 a.m. and continued working in his office until around 8:00 or 9:00 at night, six and sometimes seven days a week. The amazing part about this to me was that he never complained about it! In fact, it almost seemed to agree with him!

I didn't find out that he worked these hours on a regular basis until I had been with the company a couple of months. When I did, he assured me that the reason he worked such long hours was primarily due to his own preference—he did not expect anyone else to follow suit. That sounded good to me, especially since I didn't know how long I would be staying at this job, or if I would have to return to Holland in the near future—but I had a feeling that the corporate world would once again try to swallow me up the way previous corporate jobs had done.

It wasn't long before I found out how right I was. What had seemed like a great place to work, with a supportive boss and a reasonable work schedule was quickly turning into a sweat shop. Physical inventories were scheduled for the warehouses where the fruit was stored and office employees were expected to come in to help record the inventory counts on a weekend without any additional pay and no notice until the Thursday or Friday before.

I thought this was a little outdated to say the least. I had been willing to make these kind of sacrifices when I was in my twenties about a hundred years earlier, but at this stage of the game I felt like I, and the rest of the people in the office, deserved a little more consideration than that. Amazingly enough, damn few of the other employees seemed to complain—or if they did, they mostly mumbled under their breath and still went along with the last minute requests to work the entire weekend for free.

I started getting worried that this job was going to turn out like many I had in the past in which your whole life seems to get absorbed by your work duties. On top of that, I began to wonder how I would ever be able to get myself out of this spider's web if the time ever came when Yolande called me to tell me she couldn't come back to the U.S. for the next ten years, or she needed me to come back for an indefinite time before she could return. In either case, I would have to invent an excuse that would keep me away from my job for weeks or months at a time, and I was pretty sure the company would *not* go along with that.

I wouldn't have felt all that bad about quitting except for the burden it would put on my boss. He was just too good of a guy to leave hanging in the lurch. I started feeling really bad as we got closer and closer to the year end because the work kept piling up and deep down I knew that if I had to leave at a moment's notice to get Yo back, then that's exactly what I would do. I think most people would, but I still hated the thought of leaving my boss and the other people in my department stuck with the mess that was beginning to unfold before us.

We made it through December and we were still able to keep the reports and cash flow rolling, although it kept getting more and more difficult—especially because it was now the Christmas season when many of the office employees had scheduled their vacation time, leaving us more shorthanded than ever. We even lost one of our key people for two weeks when she returned home to the Philippines over the holidays. Unfortunately, no one else had ever been trained in her job duties, so we all had to jump in and blindly attempt to complete her reports—which would cause many problems and a lot of hair pulling on my part during the next few months.

I was working 12 hour days five days a week for the most part now, with extra hours on the weekends if needed. Although I didn't particularly enjoy working that hard, I didn't mind it as much as I might have otherwise, simply because Yo wasn't there. I had very little I really wanted to do by myself when I wasn't working, so in a way it was good. It kept me busy and kept my mind off of how much I missed her.

Of course, I still called her every weekend to find out how things were going with her. I would tell her about how many hours I and the rest of the office people were working at my job and she was amazed that anyone would work that many hours without getting any extra pay. I tried to explain that that's just the way it usually is in America when you have a salaried job—you end up working tons of overtime without getting paid anything extra for it. She thought that was basically insane, and after I thought it through, I had to agree with her.

The only reason companies can do it here is because people let them. If everyone refused to work excessive hours without extra pay, then companies would either pay them for the extra time or just wait and schedule it during normal business hours. But I know why most people do it—it's ingrained in our society. We've been brought up to believe that hard work will eventually be rewarded and that the harder people work, the more wealth and prosperity they will receive.

In many ways, that's true. If your goal is to accumulate as much wealth and material goods as you can, America is a great place to do it. You can find ways to make a lot of money, if you have the right background and/or education, but there is almost always a big price to pay in terms of time and personal freedom. Some people don't seem to mind this. They seem to think that it doesn't matter if both spouses in a family have to work 50 to 60 hours per week as long as they can have a nice house to live in, two or more nice cars to drive and all the clothes and toys their kids could possibly want. Then, of course, once the kids are old enough to go to college, the parents feel like they have a duty to pay their way, and not only that, they have to pay their way to the most prestigious, most expensive school that their children qualify for—because isn't that the American way? To make sure your kids have a better life than you had, no matter how much you have to sacrifice to achieve it?

That's the way it seems to me that most Americans justify their need to work at jobs they hate for years on end, afraid to do anything else because it wouldn't pay as well, or provide as many benefits or help them send their kids to the best colleges after they retire. I guess most people must feel it's worth it. If not, I can't even begin to understand why they would do it.

In any event, my attitude about the role work should play in a person's life, and their obligations to their children and grandchildren, etc. had long changed. At one time, I too believed that no sacrifice was too great for my family. I was willing to work myself into the ground, if that's what it took, to make sure my family had a comfortable lifestyle and we could all enjoy the comforts that could be bought by following the corporate lifestyle. However, now that my daughters were grown and on their own, I realized that there were many things I wanted out of life too, aside from just providing for others, and that I had never really tried to satisfy those needs. But once I met Yo, I realized that the materialistic lifestyle was not what I had always wanted after all.

I could easily give up owning a house. I had little need for a fancy expensive car, and I definitely had no need for a country club membership or anything along those lines. What I wanted was to be able to travel all over the world, to see new places and experience new cultures that I had never seen before.

And I didn't need to do it from a four star hotel everywhere I went. I could deal with less than comfy surroundings if it gave me a chance to experience something I never would be able to do otherwise. Fortunately, when I found Yo, I found someone who felt the same way—which is why she had a hard time understanding why the people in my company were so willing to give up so much of their lives for their job. I knew why, since I had thought the same way as them for many, many years. But now, I could see just how much I had given up and I wasn't nearly as willing to do so anymore.

Unfortunately, I really had nothing better to do except to wait to hear more news from Yo about how and when she might be coming back. So I continued working the ridiculous hours and talking to Yo for an hour or two every weekend. Until we could get more information from someone, that was basically the only thing we could do. As the year came to a close, I tried to prepare for the onslaught of year end reports that I knew would have to be done as quickly as possible after the first of the new year. After that, I hoped the workload would become more reasonable and the time pressures less intense, so that I could start trying to live a "normal" life once again. However, as far as the job was concerned, everything was about to get worse than ever—and a lot uglier.

Ironically, in the long run that turned out to be a pretty good thing after all.

LOOKING FOR MR. FALL GUY

Chapter XXIII

After I came back to the office in January things got even more hectic. This was mostly due to the year end financial reports that had to be prepared, but in addition, we were still severely understaffed, and even more critical, we were severely under capitalized.

My boss, Roy, kept assuring me that the pressure would ease up after year end, but in the meantime we had the reporting deadlines that had to be met and the daily battles with creditors who would be calling to get their bills paid. Our corporate office was taking over the bill paying function once we switched over to a new computer system in March, but right at that time, it seemed like that was a million years away.

Roy turned over the reporting duties to me and my assistant, a feisty middle aged Filipino lady who didn't like having to explain anything she did to anyone. That was what actually started the major problem for me.

She had gone back to the Philippines over the last two weeks of December to take her two week vacation over the Christmas holidays with her relatives. Unfortunately, she prepared a monthly report that reconciled the amount we owed a sister company within the same corporate organization. The problem was she had never reconciled the report to the other company's satisfaction, and now that we were preparing the year end reports all the discrepancies between the two companies had to be resolved. Since I had been given the duty of trying to reconcile the report in December while she was gone, and because she was now immersed in other year end reports, Roy asked me to try to complete it once again.

For anyone who has never worked in an accounting department for a major corporation at year end, it is hard to understand exactly how much pressure there is to get financial reports done at this time. Twelve to fifteen hour work days are the norm, and tensions become extremely high. Needless to say, it doesn't help when the company had been going through growing pains with a new corporate owner for the last 18 months. To make a long story short, I spent the better part of five long, twelve to thirteen hour days trying to get this inter-company report completed.

The balance owed had been misstated for months, and no one seemed to be able to determine how specific amounts had been entered in the records. After countless phone calls, investigation of old invoices and shipping documents and a lot of hair pulling, I thought I had determined the correct amount.

I walked into Roy's office and reviewed the report with him. By this time it was after 10:00 p.m. on the last day of our year end reporting deadline, and we were all at the end of our ropes. Roy asked me a few questions about the report and I explained as best I could. I still had some questions about specific amounts that I couldn't pin down, but it was useless to ask any questions of Linda, the Filipino lady who had prepared the report before me. Neither Roy nor I could ever understand her complicated, convoluted explanations. Yet for reasons that always eluded me, she was able to keep her job, even with her hostile, sassy attitude. In spite of all the obstacles, we finished all the year end reporting requirements on time.

Now we had to complete the monthly closing for the month of January. During this time no one worked harder than Roy. He put in even more hours than anyone else to try to help keep the company running and still try to meet the impossible deadlines imposed on us by our corporate office and outside auditors. All in all, it was an accountant's nightmare, but late in the afternoon of January 29th, we had almost completed the month end reports due for January (we had a fiscal month end instead of a calendar month end, which meant that our monthly deadlines were usually before the actual calendar month end.)

I was finally wrapping up one of the month end reports I had to complete shortly before 6:00 p.m. that afternoon, but had to have Roy's approval before I could fax it off. I looked around the office but couldn't seem to find him. I waited in my office for another twenty or thirty minutes and went searching for him again. He was nowhere to be found.

I thought this was very strange, in view of the fact that he had been staying at the office up until two or three in the morning if necessary in order to get the year end reporting done. But for some reason now, his office door was open, but he was missing for a good 45 minutes or so.

Finally I walked by his office and found him standing at his desk, shuffling some papers together. 'Roy," I said, "Have you got a minute to sign off on this report?" He had a very strange look on his face and seemed a little nervous, but he said "Sure, Michael. Just give me a couple of minutes, alright?" Then he walked out of his office. I went back to my office to unwind while I waited for him to come back.

After about twenty minutes he still hadn't returned, so I started prowling the hallways looking for him again. By now it was around 7:00 p.m. and there was hardly anyone else left in the office. I happened to walk by the corner office which belonged to Matt, the company president. Suddenly Sam, the corporate vice president who also had an office at our division was behind me. "Michael, have you got a minute?" he asked and walked into Matt's corner office.

Matt was seated behind his desk. Sam sat down in one of the seats in front of the desk and gestured for me to sit in the other chair. I knew right away something important was about to go down. These two guys didn't normally stick around into the evening hours. Nobody outside of the accounting people ever did that.

I had heard that the company was looking for someone to fill the financial vice president spot for all of the fruit companies owned by the corporation. The first thought that came into my head was that they had decided it was time to move Roy into that spot, and he was going to have to jump in immediately. I quickly assumed that the reason Sam and Matt were calling me into Matt's office was to let me know gently that Roy, who had been my mentor and buffer with the corporate office, would be needed elsewhere, and that I would have to assume his duties, at least on a temporary basis.

As soon as I sat down, Sam started talking. "Michael, you know that this is a dynamic company and we have a desperate, ongoing need for top notch leadership in all our management positions." Yep, I knew that all right. Unfortunately, Roy was probably one of the few managers in the company who could really be called "top notch."

"Well, my job is to make sure we have the right people in those management positions in this company," Sam went on. Here it comes, I thought. I was sure Sam was about to say, "Roy is being promoted to divisional financial vice president and we want you to take over as acting financial vice president for this company. "I was all set to put on a show of modesty and tell Sam and Matt how flattered I was that they wanted me to step into Roy's job.

Then Sam dropped the bomb.

"We've given this a lot of thought and we've come to the conclusion that Roy is not fulfilling the duties of financial V.P. As a result, he's been terminated and is no longer with the company."

"HUH? ROY has been TERMINATED?" I thought. Where were they ever going to find anyone else who would work as hard and put in as many hours as he did? And besides, how could he no longer be with the company? I had just seen him about fifteen minutes earlier!

I started to feel a little numb as Sam continued. "I know this must come as a shock to you," he said. "We know you worked very closely with Roy and we just want you to know we appreciate all the hard work you've done—and we need you to step up to the plate and provide leadership to the department to keep things rolling until Roy's replacement comes on board."

Well, it was a bit of a shock, all right. I didn't know exactly what to say, but for a minute or two, I still tried to play the good corporate soldier and not blurt out what I was really thinking. "Wow!", I said. "I really don't know what to say right now."

"We understand", Sam said, "and believe me, this wasn't an easy decision for me. I've lost a lot of sleep during the past few nights because of this, but I have to do what's best for this company and Roy just wasn't keeping things under control."

I knew what Sam was alluding to. The company had had a disastrous inventory reduction which caused a big hit on their financial statements at the end of the year. But I knew that wasn't Roy's fault. He had absolutely no control over the inventory reporting. I knew that, Sam knew that, and Matt knew that. It was suddenly obvious to me why they were firing Roy. They needed a scapegoat to save their own skins.

I slowly started piecing the puzzle together and wondered what the right response should be. Should I quit right then and there, or should I play along until I knew it was time to leave for Holland and bring Yolande back?

"So we need you to hang in there with us and provide the leadership we need to keep the department running over the next few weeks. Will you be able to do that?" Sam asked me.

I hate to say it, but right at that moment I took the easy way out. "Well, this is a little sudden," I started, "but I'll do whatever it takes to keep things running." I wanted to bite my tongue while I said it, but I couldn't decide what the right thing to do would be at that moment.

"Good!" Sam said as he stood up and held out his hand to me. "We knew we could depend on you!" Matt had been silent during this whole conversation, but he finally reached out his hand to me also and said something like, "Thanks for stepping up, Mike," or something like that.

I walked out of Matt's office and into my own, and sat down at my desk to try to digest what just happened. *Roy was gone!* The hardest working man I ever met, and the only manager who seemed to have a sense of humor and a dose of humanity in the whole company! And now I was being asked to "step up to the plate" and keep the department running while the wimps who ran the company picked out someone to replace Roy and save their own skins by using him as the fall guy for the inventory problems. And I basically agreed to do it!!

I felt like such a wimp! But what else was I supposed to do? I still needed a job didn't I?

Wait a minute! Maybe I *didn't* really need a job any more—at least not <u>this</u> job! I had already made arrangements to take a two week vacation in March to go back to Holland to visit Yo, who was still "running the family business while her father recuperated"! Maybe instead of a two week vacation starting on March 16th, that could be my date of termination!

Why not? I was hoping to find a way to escape from this hellhole for months without putting a bigger burden on good old Roy. Now I didn't have to worry about Roy! The company had conveniently "taken care" of that for me! I really hated what they did to him, but at the same time, it seemed like this was my golden opportunity! I could leave this job without doing any damage to Roy at all now! It was almost like God was telling me. "Here's your chance, dummy. Either take it now or don't come crying to me about being stuck in this sweat shop job!"

As I lay awake that night, I decided there was only one thing holding me back from quitting. I needed to call Yo in the morning and make sure she was in agreement with me. It was only fair. She should know about things like this before they actually happen. However, I knew deep down that she wouldn't disagree. In fact, I was sure that she would definitely agree that quitting would be the only logical thing to do. She thought I was a little crazy to have put up with it for this long!

I tried to fall asleep so I could call Yo in the morning and tell her I was quitting. Then I would go back to Holland in March and wait there until her visa was restored or go traveling somewhere else with her to find a job in another country. I rolled around for at least half the night before I finally drifted off for a couple of hours.

CUTTING THE CORD

Chapter XXIV

I called Yo the next morning around 7:00 a.m. It was 4:00 p.m. in Holland and she was just getting home from her day shift at the CD factory. I told her about what happened to Roy and how I thought that this was a signal for me to quit. She couldn't have agreed more. She thought that that was exactly how I should respond and hoped it would make the company management think twice about getting rid of valuable employees so casually. I knew that was never going to happen, but I was happy she felt the same way I did.

I got to my office around 8:00 a.m. I walked to the corner office where Sam worked when he was at the division. I heard him talking on the phone to someone, so I stood outside and waited. I didn't bother to go to my office first and take off my jacket. I figured that once he heard what I had to say, he'd probably tell me to take off and never come back anyway.

I waited about ten minutes for him to finish his conversation. While I waited I paced nervously back and forth in front of his door. The only other person in the office that early was Joe, our freight manager, and as I looked up I saw him watching me, wondering what was going on. I didn't say anything, but just kept pacing back and forth, waiting for Sam to get off the phone.

Finally the conversation ended. I walked into Sam's office and said, "Excuse me, Sam, have you got a minute?" He looked a little surprised, but said "Sure." I sat down and started to give the speech I had rehearsed driving over in my car.

"I've been thinking about everything that happened yesterday. You said you didn't get much sleep for the last few nights thinking about your decision, and I didn't get much last night thinking about mine."

He stared at me, wondering what I was going to say next. I handed him the resignation letter I had already typed. "I feel that Roy was unjustly terminated yesterday for things that he didn't have any control over, and to make a long story short, in good conscience, I don't feel that I can continue to work for this company any longer."

He stopped to look at the resignation letter I just handed him in disbelief. I continued my final commentary, expecting him to throw me out of the office any second now. "I'm giving you a termination date of March 16th—that's when I was planning on going back to Holland on vacation to visit my wife anyway—but if you want me gone sooner, I can be out the door in five minutes."

He actually smiled at this last part, and said "No, Mike, we definitely don't want you gone any sooner." Then to my surprise, instead of acting upset, he was philosophical.

"I know you think Roy was being held responsible for things that he couldn't control, but he wasn't. Everything he was held responsible for was within his control," Sam said. "There's a lot of things that have happened that you don't know about, and I'm not about to go into now, but if this is your decision, I respect it. You have to do what you think is right, and I have to do what I think is right for this company. Believe me, it wasn't an easy decision to make, but like it or not, that's my job and in this case, that's what I felt I had to do."

He almost had me believing he did something noble. But I knew beyond the shadow of a doubt that Roy had been fired because of the inventory devaluation, and I also knew that only Sam and his assistant had been involved in doing that. Of course, he would try to push it off on Roy, but in this case I knew Roy absolutely did *not* control it. He had complained to me often enough about not being able to do so! So as much as Sam wanted me to believe otherwise, I knew this was just all part of the rationalization behind letting Roy go.

As I slowly realized that Sam wasn't going to throw me out on the spot, I started to relax. He finally looked up from his desk, which he had been staring at while giving his justification speech. "So when are you planning on leaving?" he asked again.

"March 16th," I said. "That's when I was planning on taking my vacation to go back to Holland to visit my wife. Only now, it looks like it just might be more permanent than that."

It all took a little over five minutes. I had given Sam my resignation letter, given him my little speech and politely waited for his rebuttal. He ended the conversation by telling me he would inform Jack, the new divisional VP who had been brought in over Roy to "reorganize" the company, and he would also let Human Resources know. I told him I already had a copy of my letter ready for the HR manager. He thanked me for giving him as much notice as I had, and I left his office.

Amazingly enough, I hadn't been asked to leave on the spot, so I walked back to my office to start to serve out the remaining month and a half of my sentence. I hadn't been in it for five minutes when Jack, the new divisional VP walked in. He sat down in my chair and said, "Morning, Mike. I just wanted to ask you how you felt about what happened with Roy yesterday?"

If ever there was an opportunity to unload on someone this was it. I didn't know Jack very well since he had only been around for a few days, but he seemed like he was sincerely trying to smooth over an ugly situation. I decided to be direct.

"I think he got screwed," I said.

"Do you?" he asked, getting ready to give me his rationale as to why it had to be done.

I didn't give him the chance. "Yeah, I do," I said, handing him my resignation letter, "and I just gave Sam my termination letter as a result."

He looked stunned. I knew that he was probably thinking the same thing Sam had been thinking a few minutes earlier. "This isn't the way this was supposed to go! Now we have to get a replacement for this guy too!"

I told him how I felt that Roy had been unjustly terminated and that I had no desire to work for the company anymore. He listened quietly and said, "Well, that's too bad. I was hoping you could be part of helping us get the company moving in a new direction here." No thank you, I thought. I had no intention to have anything to do with the new direction I saw unfolding before me. He told me he would call a meeting for the rest of the department to let them know what was going on. Then he also thanked me for giving as much notice as I did and left.

I sat there for a few minutes wondering what lay ahead of me now. Here I was, giving up a well paying job for an unknown future, not knowing where I would be working or living after the next couple of months. I wondered if I hadn't been too rash—but after a few seconds I realized that any company that could treat someone like Roy the way they did would have no loyalty or compassion for anyone else. Did I really need money that badly to be part of the heartless corporate world that would do something like that?

The answer was no. Thankfully, I would be able to live for at least a few months without worrying about where my next check was coming from. Not indefinitely, mind you, but at least until I could go back to Holland and decide what Yo and I would be doing the rest of our lives after that.

I started shuffling through the papers and organizing my day, getting ready to finish out the last month and a half of my career with the fruit company. I was already thinking about what Yo would say when I called her the next morning to tell her the results of my showdown. I could almost hear her laughing already.

SHOWDOWN AT THE CASINO BAR

Chapter XXV

As I expected, Yo thought it was a terrific way to end my fruit company job. She thought I handled it exactly the way I should have and even thought I was a little too nice about it by giving them so much notice. But I knew that I'd still be needing money at some point, so I might as well make as much as I could before I ran off to Europe to see her again. Besides, once I knew I would be leaving as of a certain date, it made the place a lot easier to stand.

For the next few days, most of the women who "reported" to me came into my office to tell me how terrible they felt because I was leaving. I knew that the main reason for this was because they were all worried about what kind of company jerk they might get next for a boss.

The one thing that I was not going to change, no matter what happened at the job was the two day trip I had planned to go to Laughlin, Nevada at the end of the week to meet my old buddy Curt. Curt was my friend from New Lenox, Illinois, where I lived for ten years. He and I had been friends for over 20 years, and I had been planning to meet him in Laughlin for about two or three months. I was really looking forward to spending a couple of days at the casinos with him, playing blackjack, hitting the buffets and telling lots of bad jokes over cheap cocktails.

Of course, after Roy got canned, good old Jack called a meeting the next day to tell everyone that we would be taking a physical inventory that weekend, and he expected all the office employees to come in to help get it recorded and summarized by Monday, without any extra pay. As soon as the meeting was over, I marched into his office to tell him I couldn't do it because I had a "family reunion" trip planned to Laughlin that was arranged months ago and I wasn't going to be able to reschedule it now.

I didn't have any intention of missing my two day holiday that I had been looking forward to for weeks. I had requested these two days as vacation days well over a month ago, when Curt first told me he would be in Laughlin the last week of January. I wasn't about to change my plans now, especially since I wouldn't be staying there more than another month or so anyway. Jack mumbled something about having to take care of it if I couldn't do it, but he understood. Good. I wasn't about to bend over backwards to try to help Jack at this point. I was going to Laughlin on Thursday!

I left work at about 5:30 Thursday afternoon and started on my long drive across the desert. The biggest problem was getting out of the L.A. area during rush hour of course. That would add at least 2 hours to the trip, but of course, I couldn't leave any earlier. There were still a lot of last minute problems to deal with, even though I had already given my notice. So I drove onto the 610 freeway to sit in stop and go traffic for a couple of hours before I got past Riverside.

I stopped for dinner somewhere around Barstow. By this time it was well after 8:00 p.m. and the traffic was finally beginning to move at a normal pace, but I had to have something to eat. I called Curt on my cell phone to tell him I was on my way. He sounded really glad that I could make it and told me to call him when I was a half hour away.

I got to the Laughlin exit off Interstate 40 around 11:00 p.m. I called Curt again to let him know I was 15 or 20 minutes away. At least, that's what I thought. I didn't realize following the curving desert road to Laughlin would take over a half an hour before I finally reached the city limits. But I knew once I got there I could relax and have a good time for at least two days. I wandered into the Mardi Gras hotel about 11:45 and headed for the blackjack table where Curt told me he would be.

I finally tracked him down at one of the blackjack tables nursing a drink and losing money. His hair was almost totally white now, which was a little bit of a shock. He had been mostly gray the last time I saw him, but still had enough dark hair left so that you really couldn't tell his age. Now he was just starting to look as old as he was, and it made me realize I probably was too.

"Mikey!" he called out once he saw me. We gave each other the high five and I sat down next to him to try my luck at the table. We sat and babbled for about two hours before we finally decided we had both lost enough money to the dealer and wandered over to the casino bar.

Curt and I talked about everything we had been doing the last three years. He had a new job selling pre-fabricated doors for a home improvements company. I told him about my latest adventure with my job. He smiled as he listened to my story and slowly shook his head. "You change jobs faster than I can keep track of them," he laughed.

After several drinks and using up all of our best jokes on the bartender, we started talking about Yolande's status. I told Curt about how Yolande was now waiting to hear from the Department of Homeland Security in Frankfurt, Germany before we would know how much longer it would take before she would be allowed to return. Curt shook his head with a disgusted look on his face and said. "You know, it's so stupid the way the government handles things like that in this country. They put your wife in jail for seven weeks and kick her out of the country, but they let all the Mexicans in for free and don't do anything about it."

I knew from my personal visit to the detention center in El Paso and from the fact that Yolande told me that 90% of her fellow detainees were Hispanic that this wasn't true. I felt the need to try to set Curt straight for some reason.

"They don't *let* them in, Curt," I told him. "They put them in jail, just like they did to Yolande if they catch them."

"That's not what I'm talking about," he said. "They keep letting all these illegal Mexicans over the border and don't do anything to stop them."

Now I was starting to get annoyed. What did he mean, they don't do anything to stop them? Some of the women Yolande had been with in the detention center had been locked up for over a year waiting to get deported. Wasn't that punishment enough in itself? What did he think the government should do, shoot them on sight? I couldn't stop myself from trying to make him understand just how harshly people who came here illegally were treated, as well as those who committed the crime of staying longer than they should, like Yo. That was when the discussion started to take an unexpected and very unpleasant turn.

"They don't *let* them come in, Curt," I told him again.

"Yeah, they do!" he replied.

"No, they don't! If they get caught, they put them in a detention center, just like they did with Yolande!"

"Yeah, but they don't do anything to stop them from coming over!"

"Well, what are we supposed to do, build a fence around the entire country?" I asked.

"YES!" Curt answered.

I was momentarily stunned. I couldn't believe he was serious.

"How is it hurting anyone if these people come to this country trying to find a better way of life and do the jobs no one else wants to do?"

"They're breaking the law. We have laws for a reason. You can't just come to a country and move in without obeying its laws!"

"Yes you can, when the law doesn't make any *sense*!" I answered. "When someone is doing more good than harm, doing jobs no one else will do, why would you make them leave?"

By now we were both getting a little bit loud, especially me. I have a tendency to get very excited when I start talking about something I feel strongly about. Some people even call it yelling. In fact, I went through a period of my life when I was something of a "rageaholic" who couldn't control his temper at all. It was actually one of the main reasons my first marriage of 21 years ended in divorce. I had been to counseling since then and had pretty much eliminated those tendencies from my personality, but every once in a while, when I started talking about something I felt passionately about, it crept back in. This was going to be one of those times.

As we continued to argue I got louder and louder. Pretty soon most of the other people in the casino bar were looking at me, wondering what Curt and I were yelling about, although I didn't realize this at the time. I wasn't even actually aware I was yelling. I really thought I was simply arguing, and "stating my case emphatically." I had no idea I was getting so loud that other people could hear what I was saying over the noise of the casino.

"If people come here looking for a better way of life, they don't commit any crimes, they don't hurt anyone else, why shouldn't they be allowed to stay if they're willing to pay any taxes due?" I asked. "How are they hurting anybody if they're performing services that have to be done, but no one else wants to do them, and if they're willing to pay whatever taxes are due? Why should they have to leave?" I continued, trying to make Curt see the other side of the argument.

"Mike," he said to me. "If someone broke into your house and moved in without you asking them there, would you let them stay?"

"But they're not moving into a *house*, Curt! They're moving into a country where they find their own places to stay and they don't make anyone else leave to live somewhere else!"

By now, we were both getting really loud, but I was still the one who was the loudest. Curt had stood up from his barstool and was now standing in front of me, arguing his case like a prosecuting attorney. I could feel myself starting to lose control, so I tried to calm down and ignore the amazing, uncompassionate, almost hateful comments I was hearing from someone who I thought was one of my best friends. I couldn't believe he could be so heartless and uncaring about people, whether they were here legally or illegally.

This was not the man I had become friends with over twenty years earlier. That man was a true optimist—friendly, happy go lucky, with an attitude that could never be broken. No matter what happened, Curt could always make a joke about it, and never let anything get him down. But now, I was talking to a man who had absolutely no concern for anyone who dared to come across our border trying to improve their life if they didn't follow governmental procedures to the letter.

I could understand having this type of animosity towards people who committed crimes, or tried to freeload on society without doing any work in return. But for the most part, that's not the kind of people who were in the detention center in El Paso with Yolande. They were simply people who wanted to have a better life for themselves and their children, and got caught up in the bureaucracy while trying to do it. They definitely weren't evil, and didn't deserve the punishment of detention—just like Yolande didn't deserve being detained and deported for failing to follow bureaucratic regulations. At least that was how I saw it. Curt unfortunately did not agree with me.

Curt was getting more animated and louder now too. I was actually trying to drop the subject because I realized we were both getting far too passionate in our arguments. I tried to turn away from him and finish my drink, but he wasn't going to let me go.

"What about the terrorists who come into this country illegally?" he demanded. "You want to let them in too?"

"No, of course not!" I said. "If anyone comes here to commit a crime, they should be thrown in jail and prosecuted, just like anyone who was *born* here and commits a crime!" I was getting more than a little irritated that he would ask me such a stupid question. "But if all they do is come here without paperwork, I don't think they should be thrown in jail for that! Why not give them an option to pay any of the taxes they owe, and then let them keep doing whatever job they're doing that no one else wants to do?"

Curt was standing in front of me now with the most serious look on his face that I'd ever seen. "Every country has laws that you have to abide by if you want to live there. If you don't abide by the laws you have to leave!" he said. Now I felt like he was lecturing me like a kid. He had the same type of look on his face as a father telling his son that he had to go to school the next day, whether he liked it or not. I couldn't take any more. Being lectured by another adult is one thing I can not stand.

"No you **DON'T**!" I shouted. "If the laws are **MORALLY WRONG**, you have a duty **NOT** to obey them!"

I must have really blasted him at this point, because instead of saying anything else, Curt just tossed his hands up in the air, turned around and walked away. I sat there for a few moments not knowing what to do.

I thought I should try to run after him and ask him to forget the whole thing and go back to just having a good time for a day or so, like we had planned. But I couldn't do that. I couldn't pretend that it really didn't matter. Obviously it did matter, to both of us. Unfortunately we were on opposite ends of the spectrum. I watched him walk off toward the elevators and wondered if he would cool off and come back.

Suddenly I could feel the eyes of several people at the bar watching me. Apparently, Curt and I had put on quite a show for the patrons there. I suddenly felt very embarrassed, not for what I had said, but for the way I had said it. I had let my emotions get the better of me and now everyone around me was watching me quietly, wondering if I was some kind of crazed lunatic that they should be afraid of.

An older Hispanic woman who had been sitting a few seats away from us had obviously heard part of the argument, and felt obliged to chime in on the subject. "Your friend was right!" she said to me. "You shouldn't allow people into this country if they're not willing to follow the law."

"Not her too!" I thought. "But if they haven't broken any laws and they're not harming anyone, and they're willing to take jobs no one else wants to do, why shouldn't we let them STAY here?" I countered.

I must have still been in my ultra loud mode without even knowing it, because at this point a Hispanic man who had been sitting across the bar from me, watching the whole debate called over to me. "You don't have to shout at us, mister! We're not deaf, you know!"

At this point I finally realized just how loud I must have been and how I must have looked to everyone around me. I got even more embarrassed but felt like I had to stay there and finish my drink, just in case Curt decided to come back. I apologized to everyone around me and told them I didn't realize I had been shouting. They said they understood, but just to try to calm down a little.

I tried to take their advice and told the lady who had started talking to me about how I probably was a little more sensitive about the subject than I should be because of what Yolande had been through. She seemed to be a little understanding, but at the same time she acted like she wanted to concentrate more on the video poker game she was playing than what I was saying.

While I talked, I kept looking toward the elevators to see if Curt was coming back. After a half hour I realized he definitely wasn't. I finally got up from the bar to make my way up to my room.

I started wondering if we had just gone through the end of our friendship. I couldn't help but think how ironic it was, that I had driven for nearly six hours to get there to relax and have a good time, and within three hours I had probably just ended a friendship of over twenty years.

It was after 3:00 a.m. now. Curt had mentioned that he would be coming down to the hotel restaurant for breakfast around 8:30 the next morning before we started on our great debate. I set my alarm for 8:00 a.m. and tried to go to sleep. Strangely enough, I still wasn't tired. My adrenaline had gotten so pumped up that it would take a while before I could relax. I tossed and turned for an hour or more before I finally drifted off.

The next morning I woke up a little before 8:00 and tried to call Curt's cell phone. He didn't answer so I left a message. "Hey, Curt, it's Mike. Listen I'm sorry I got a little over excited last night. I didn't mean to get that loud. Nobody deserves to be yelled at about their beliefs, including you. So I apologize for losing control. I hope we can still get together today the way we planned. I know you said you would be going down to the restaurant around 8:30, so I'm going to be down there about that time too. I'll be looking for you and Eileen if you still want to join me. I hope I'll see you there."

I went down to the hotel restaurant and had breakfast. Curt didn't show up. I kept looking around the restaurant, but when I left around 9:15, he was nowhere to be found. I called his cell phone again. Still no answer. I left another message telling him I would be at the black jack tables waiting for him if he still wanted to get together.

I walked over to the black jack tables where I had met him about 10 hours earlier and sat down to play for a while. I won and lost, won and lost several hands. Still no Curt. I looked at my watch. It was after 10:30 now, and I still hadn't heard from him. I knew this probably meant that I wouldn't hear from him again that day—or maybe ever again. It must have been a more serious debate than I even realized. I went up to my room to get my bags and check out.

Reluctantly, I got in my car and started on the drive back to Long Beach. As I drove back through the bright desert sunshine, I couldn't help but think about how my life had again taken such a weird, unexpected turn. I thought I was going to Laughlin to unwind from the pressures of a horrible job situation and relax with one of my best friends. Instead, I was driving back home after spending only three hours with my friend and possibly ending a twenty year old friendship.

I wondered if I would ever have anything resembling a "normal" life again.

THE END OF THE INCREDIBLE JOURNEY

Chapter XXVI

When I was about halfway back to Long Beach, Curt finally called me on my cell phone. I pulled over to the side of Interstate 40 to take the call.

"Mike," Curt said, "Are you still here?"

"No," I answered.

"Listen, I'm sorry I didn't call you back, but in all honesty I didn't know what to say. I didn't know how we could talk to each other today after last night. You know, it would be like a white elephant in the room that nobody wanted to say anything about. So I took the easy way out and just didn't answer you. But you were the bigger man than me, you apologized and I should have been willing to talk to you about it, but I just didn't know what to say."

I didn't really know what to say at that point either. I told him I was sorry that I got so excited and I didn't really know how loud I was getting, but that obviously it was a subject we both felt pretty strongly about, and unfortunately we were on opposite sides. He did say that if he had thought about it more, he probably would have realized how personal the whole subject was to me, and that maybe if it was *his* wife who had to spend seven weeks in a detention center and got deported for overstaying her visa here, he might feel a little differently about it.

"*Exactly*!" I thought. "That's *just* what I was trying to tell you!"

I told him I was surprised that it had gotten so far out of control and said I never thought that we would have such a huge argument about anything that it would cause me to lose a good friend. He said not to worry, that I hadn't lost a friend and that the whole issue would just be a subject we would have to make sure we both avoided in the future. But I knew right then that it would never be the same kind of friendship again. We were too far apart on the political spectrum. From that day on we would never trust each other completely or feel the same way about each other again.

We both hung up and I continued driving back to Long Beach. When I was about an hour away, I finally realized that I hadn't slept more than about three hours the previous night. The early afternoon traffic was already starting to get bogged down as I drove into metropolitan L.A. and I was having a hard time staying awake. I pulled over into the parking lot of a truck stop somewhere near Ontario and took a nap.

By the time I got back to Long Beach it was already early evening. I went into my apartment, unpacked my bags and fell into a deep sleep for the rest of the night. When I woke up I wondered what else could happen in the series of unfortunate incidents that Yo and I had been through since that fateful day at White Sands.

The next morning I called Yo to tell her all about the events in Laughlin. She was astounded to hear about how my casual discussion with Curt had turned into a potentially friendship ending argument, but she understood exactly how I felt. She was surprised and disappointed that Curt would have such a harsh, uncompassionate viewpoint, just as I was. However, she sympathized with me and said that Curt and I would probably still be friends, but not the same way we had been before.

Then she dropped the bomb.

She had gotten a letter from the Department of Homeland Security the day before. Her visa had been reinstated!

She was able to come back to the U.S.!!!

I couldn't believe it! Just a few minutes before I was telling her how lousy and depressed I felt after the incident with Curt in Laughlin, and now here she was telling me that we could be reunited again within a matter of weeks! The saga was nearly over!

We quickly decided that since I was now free of my job with the fruit company, that when I came to see her in Holland in March, that I would now be staying for a month's vacation instead of two weeks. She had even gone so far as to plan two mini trips for us while I was there—one to the Dutch island of Texel and a ten day trip to Egypt!

I almost couldn't believe this was really happening. Not only was I ecstatic about being able to see Yo and bring her back to the U.S. with me, now I would be going on a trip to two places that sounded like they would be lots of fun! Texel was an island in the North Sea that offered three quiet days of biking and exploration of the shops and restaurants that populated it, and Egypt was a place I had never expected to go to. My dad had been stationed there during World War Two, and I had pictures of him riding a camel in front of the Pyramids. I told Yo right then that if we were going to Egypt, that I had to have a picture of me riding a camel in front of the Pyramids too, just like my dad. Of course she agreed.

Now the hardest part was having to wait another month and a half before I got to see her. The next day was the day of the Super Bowl and I had already made plans to join my daughter and my first ex-wife and her husband at their house in Oceanside to watch the Super Bowl with them.

I thought the most exciting part of that day would be to cheer my beloved Chicago Bears on in their first Super Bowl appearance in twenty one years, but now the most exciting thing was to share the news with everyone. They were all excited and happy for me too. In fact, it was good to have some pleasant news to talk about since the Bears played horrendously and ended up losing to the Indianapolis Colts by a big margin.

The next six weeks seemed to drag by. I would call Yo every four or five days to let her know about how the transition was being handled at my job (poorly), and tried to get all the loose ends tied up before I made my journey back to Holland again. I finally finished all the primary duties that had to be completed and was ready to take my final personal days off two days before I left for Holland.

I made the flight from L.A. to New York and then to Amsterdam again, very much like I had done the previous two times I went there. It was starting to become a routine by now. I was very glad that it wasn't nearly as suspenseful as the first time I had flown there, wondering if Yo would be following on the next flight over from Atlanta.

I got my bags form the baggage carousel after I landed and went out to find Yo in the Arrivals area of Schiopol Airport. She was right where she said she'd be this time, and when I saw her she came up to me and said "Hoi!." Then we had the predictable long, passionate smooch that we had both been saving for over eight months.

I'd like to say that there was some incredible climactic ending to this story after all we had been through, but the truth is, after Yo told me she had been approved to come back to the U.S., everything else was pretty anti-climactic. We went to Texel and had three fun days of exploring the island by bike and taking lots of pretty pictures. Then it was on to Egypt, where I finally got to have my picture taken, with Yo, on top of a camel in front of the Pyramids, just like my dad.

The only negative thing about the whole trip this time was that I just couldn't deal with the Egyptian merchants' enthusiasm for harassing tourists. They seem to think that the more they hassle you, the more likely you are to buy something from them. For me, it was just the opposite. The more they chattered at me, the more annoyed I got, and I actually ended up yelling at a couple of them before they would stop. I actually dreaded having to walk anywhere in Egypt except when we were with a guide on one of our tours of the temples and pyramids. Yo didn't seem to mind, of course, but I wasn't able to ignore the incessant jabbering and street confrontations the way she could, so it was not a completely pleasant trip from my perspective. The bottom line to me was I loved the Egyptian temples and ruins, but could easily do without most of the Egyptians merchants.

Regardless of how much the Egyptian merchants may have annoyed me, the one thing that wasn't going to change was that Yo was coming back to Long Beach with me. After we got back to her parents' house in Uden, there was a small going away party in their back yard the day before we left. Yo's brother, Bart and his wife, Dees were there along with a few other friends that Yo had worked with or grew up with. Some of them did not feel inclined to speak much English, so my conversations were limited to Bart and Dees, and the husband of one of Yo's friends who didn't seem to mind not speaking Dutch for a little while.

The next day we were up early to get in Yo's parents car and have Rieke drive us to the train station. Rieke waited for the train with us, and just before it arrived she told me that she was "glad that Yo had a man to be with in America now." I looked at Yo and she was just as surprised as I was. Rieke was an extremely strong willed feminist who had taught her daughters that they didn't need to have a man in their lives to be happy, but here she was telling me how glad she was that Yo would be with me while she was in the U.S. ! I guess when it comes to your own daughter, even feminists tend to be a little protective.

The train finally came and we all said our goodbyes. First Yo and Rieke gave each other the customary three Dutch kisses and then Rieke and I did the same thing. We gave each other big hugs and waved goodbye as we got on the train. Yo had packed our bags and we had our tickets for the plane. Most importantly, we both had passports and she had a visa that allowed her to come back to the U.S. with me.

It had been a long, long journey—one that I wasn't sure would ever really be resolved at times—but we had finally made it through to the end. We were coming back to America! The saga was officially over!

As we pulled out of the train station, a feeling of relief and confidence slowly came over me. After all we had been through, we were finally headed back where we started together. Now we were ready for *anything*.

Deep down inside, my gut feeling was:

<u>BRING IT ON</u>!!!!!!

Aftermath:
STRANGE DAYS INDEED!

I finished the first draft of this book shortly before Christmas, 2007. I wanted Yo to be the first one to read it because I knew she would be able to make some corrections about when things happened, in what sequence, and to remind me about any important incidents I might have left out. I let her review it and made the corrections which she was able to point out to me.

During her review, she gave me more information about her experience in the detention center at El Paso. Some of them have already been mentioned previously in this book, but there were several things that I left out. I wanted to add them here to give everyone a clear picture of just how inefficient the whole process was—whether you feel it was justified or not.

The first clue as to how slow and pedantic the process of incarceration would be was that it took the Border Patrol intake agents almost four hours just to get Yo's required information input into their computer system. On top of that, although she finally arrived at the detention center around midnight on the day she was picked up in White Sands around 10:00 a.m., she had to wait until approximately 4:00 am to receive clothes, shoes and a pillowcase. During this time, she had to wait in an unheated room and lie on the floor while she was forced to listen to extremely loud, blaring rock music from a guard's radio.

Before she was allowed to enter the barracks, she had to take a physical exam. The nurse who examined her told her that her blood pressure was slightly higher than normal and told her she should take some pills to control it. Yo replied that the only reason her blood pressure might be high could be that she was forced to lie on the floor all night long, listening to extremely loud music in an unheated room, and she refused to take the pills on principle. However, the nurse still noted that she had high blood pressure and Yo eventually had to make two more visits to the facility doctor as a result. He eventually agreed that the increase noted in her blood pressure was not significant and decided she did not need the pills anyway.

She was taken to the barracks at 7:00 a.m. where she was left in front of the barracks door and told to knock. She did so several times, but did not get any answer.

Finally after about 15 minutes, a guard came to the door and asked her what she was doing there! She answered that she was a new "guest," and then it took another 20 minutes or so before they finally let her come in!

For some reason she did not get a pillow when she was checked in. She assumed she would have one waiting for her at her bed, but when she didn't she asked one of the guards how she could get one. The guard told her she was an "afternoon guard," and that she would have to ask the "morning guard" about it the next day. She did exactly what she was told, but again, for some unknown reason, it took another 5 days before she got her pillow!

All of the detainees were given a booklet to read when they were admitted, spelling out all the rules and regulations of the detention center. In the book, Yo noted that one of the rules stated that no detainee is allowed to wear clothing with holes, and if they did so "reprisals" could take place. However, each time she was issued one of the standard gray sweatshirts given to the detainees, she noticed they all had at least one three inch hole in them. She brought this up to the guards each time, but was then told she had to take whatever she was given. So much for official regulations!

The days followed a very routine schedule, as you might expect in a prison. Lights came on every morning at 5:30 a.m. Breakfast was served at 6:30 a.m. three times a week, but for some unknown reason, twice a week the male detainees were served breakfast at 6:30 and the female detainees had to wait until 8:00. Why they varied it like this, no one knew.

After breakfast, the women settled down in the barracks to watch TV, which always featured the latest videos from the Mexican hit parade. At 8:30, two of the detainees would clean the barracks. They were paid $1.00 per day for this service, as were the women who volunteered for kitchen jobs, outside cleaning and laundry work. All of the other women in the barracks would sit on their beds and stay off the floor until the cleaning was over.

At 9:45 a.m. the morning count took place. All the doors were closed and the guards would count all of the women in the barracks three times. This usually took approximately 45 minutes, but if there were any discrepancies among the counts it could last as long as an hour and a half. While they were being counted, the women were told to sit on their beds and stay *silent,* or as "De Kleine" usually said it, ***"SILENCIO!"***

If the count went smoothly, lunch was served at 11:00 a.m. then the women would have 1 hour to walk around outside the barracks on an asphalt playground if it wasn't raining, or too windy, or too hot or too cold. At 2:00 p.m. there was another count, again with all of the women sitting on their beds, silently waiting for the all clear from the guards once it was finally finished. At 4:00 p.m.—yes, 4:00 p.m.—they had dinner, and at 6:45 p.m. yet *another* count had to be done!

The uniform which Yo had to wear consisted of "grandma" underpants (as she described them), which were two sizes too large, a sports bra which was so small that it rode up and exposed her boobs any time she raised her arms, dark blue pants which were way too large and a sleeveless shirt, similar to a surgical smock. She had to keep all her clothes under her mattress for the first three weeks until she got her own locker. After that, she still had to keep her shoes on the bed because keeping anything *under* the bed was a big no-no.

When she finally got her locker, it took 3 guards to complete the transaction. One guard would yell out the detainees' names and locker numbers. The other guard would watch a third guard to see if the key for that locker number fit the lock. They assigned 7 or 8 lockers at a time this way, and with 3 guards performing the ceremony for each detainee, it would take approximately 45 minutes to complete.

One of the detainees was a woman from Lithuania, and when it came time for her to get sent back to Lithuania, she discovered that a silver bracelet and two cell phones were missing from the detainees' central storage "depot." When none of the guards could explain what happened to them, she contacted the Lithuanian consulate. Her consulate told her not to leave until the items were found. Strangely enough, after the Lithuanian consulate contacted the facility's authorities, the missing bracelet and cell phones suddenly materialized, and the woman left to return to Lithuania with her boyfriend.

Shortly before Yo was able to leave El Paso, a "high ranking official" from ICE came to the barracks to answer the detainees' questions. No one seemed to know exactly what his title was and what exactly he planned to do about any complaints they might have, but since he came into the barracks and sat down to take questions, they figured they might as well ask him what they wanted to know. Yo, of course, was not at all shy about asking the official some questions.

First she asked the official why they could not have some DVDs of movies more suitable for women on the barracks TV, instead of the violent films and car chase epics that seemed to be the primary fare supplied for them by the guards every day. The barracks actually cheered when she asked the question, so it was definitely something most of the women were concerned with. The official said the center was in the process of getting more DVDs oriented towards women, and that he thought it was a good question.

She also asked why the male detainees' barracks had two TVs—one for English programs and one for Spanish—while the women detainees had only one. (The official didn't even ask how they knew this, but of course, it was something they had all heard through the "grapevine.") The answer was that the two TVs were needed for the males to keep them from becoming disgruntled and potentially violent. Yo responded that that was fine, but the women deserved two TVs in their barracks just as much as the men did! (Whether or not any of these complaints ever did any good is something she didn't stay long enough to find out.)

Next Yo was asked to serve as an interpreter for two Chinese girls in the barracks who had a question about changing one of the women's plea to stay in the United States to a plea to be sent back to China because she recently found out that her long lost husband, whom she thought was dead, was recently seen in China. One of the women asked the question in Chinese, and the second woman translated to Yo in broken English. Somehow Yo was able to understand the second woman's translation and re-phrase it for the official to understand. The official listened to Yo's question and basically told them that they could do what the Chinese girl wanted, but that she would not be able to go back to China until they could get enough Chinese detainees to justify sending a plane there from America. Unfortunately for the Chinese girl, Yo didn't think that would happen anytime soon.

Finally Yo asked the official, the most important question from her personal viewpoint: "Why was it," she asked,"that I knew that I would be deported within 3 days after I was picked up by the Border Patrol, but it has taken over 6 weeks to get a plane ticket and my travel papers prepared to send me back to Holland?"

The official responded at first by guessing that the delay was due to the time it took to schedule a court hearing, but then Yo reminded him that in the case of European detainees, they did not have a court hearing before they were sent back to their native country. She then asked him, "If you're in such a hurry to kick us out, why does it take 6 weeks to get it done?"

When he heard this, the official just looked at her for a moment. Then he laughed and said he didn't know, but he agreed that it seemed like a long time to get the problem resolved. In short, he didn't really give them any definite answers to any of their questions, but at least he made them feel like someone was listening to their complaints and concerns—if only for a day.

One other sidebar to the official's visit was particularly gratifying. While the official was talking to the detainees, the guard known as "De Kleine" started to make a big show of picking up the telephone and listening to it, as if she was checking it for something. She did this two or three times while the official was talking, which created a major distraction. Finally, the official stopped talking to the detainees and turned to De Kleine and asked "Do you check the phones like this every day, or is this just being done because I'm here?" De Kleine was so embarrassed at being "outed" in front of the detainees like this that she simply walked out of the room without saying anything, much to the detainees' delight.

Although being stuck in the detention center for nearly seven weeks was no picnic, it was still a shorter sentence than a lot of other women had to serve. Most of the Mexican or Central American women who were there had to stay at least 60 days at a minimum, some of them as long as a year.

There were two women in their early twenties there from Ethiopia who fled the war raging in their country. Both of their parents had already been killed in the war and they did not know if their brothers were still alive or not. They entered the U.S. illegally, but they went to the U.S. embassy shortly after arriving here to ask for political asylum. Their reward for trusting in the U.S. government was that at the time of Yo's arrival in El Paso, they had already spent 10 months in the detention center waiting for a decision on their ability to stay in the United States.

One of the women there happened to be born in Mexico only because her mother went into labor while visiting friends across the border from El Paso. She had four other siblings in her family, but she was the only one who was not a natural born U.S. citizen. At 28 years old, she had lived in the U.S. all her life and even had a 7 year old daughter who was a U.S. citizen. The reason she never got a visa to become a U.S. citizen resulted from the fact that her parents had divorced when she was very young, and her father later died while she was still a child. Although she tried, she could not obtain her father's birth certificate from the Mexican government. One day she was involved in a domestic dispute with her husband. The police were called in and during their investigation they discovered she never got her visa. The next thing she knew she was in the El Paso detention center.

While she was in exile in Holland, Yo saw a story on Dutch television about a Dutch woman who had been picked up by the Border Patrol along with her husband because they too had overstayed their visas—by a grand total of *ten days*! The reason they had overstayed was simply because they were on a nationwide tour of America and the husband had gotten ill while in Chicago for a week. They were in the process of crossing the border to go into Mexico when they got stopped. The interesting part about this story is that the husband ended up in *solitary confinement* for *4 weeks* in a real prison outside of El Paso!

For reasons which were never explained to them, the couple was taken to the El Paso detention center like any other detainees, but after just one day there they were both sent to full scale *prisons* in El Paso! The husband, who we'll call Wally, had been questioned by the jail personnel after his arrival there, and somehow a question came up in which he was asked if he had ever had any thoughts of suicide. He responded truthfully that, yes, he had, as a teenager for some reason, but that that was all in the past and he never had any thoughts like that anymore.

That was all it took for him to be put in solitary confinement for four weeks! Altogether he ended up spending 6 weeks in detention before being sent back to Holland and she spent 8. This was such a bizarre situation that it was highlighted as a special news story in Holland. Naturally, the Dutch people who watched it thought the whole thing was incredibly ridiculous. Unfortunately it was more routine than unusual when it came to the treatment of detainees at El Paso.

There was also the Christian woman from Asia that was discussed earlier, who was seeking asylum from political enemies in her native country. Christians were treated like second class citizens in her native country, and routinely persecuted because of their faith.

The woman had given her nephew a raincoat to wear. This would seem to be an innocent enough act, but because her nephew had protested the govern-ment's policies towards Christians, he was considered an enemy of the government and therefore a "terrorist"—and by lending him a raincoat, she was considered a terrorist too!

She had fled to Hong Kong and then Mexico to escape interrogation and probable torture by her country's government. Once she got to Mexico, she crossed the border into El Paso and voluntarily turned herself in to the U.S. Border Patrol to seek political asylum. However, when she could not produce a valid passport or other legal documentation from her home country, she was picked up as an illegal immigrant and sent to the detention center!

Although she was an illegal immigrant, she was also a political refugee who was fighting extradition back to Asia to avoid being tortured and/or killed when she returned because of her "terrorist" activities. However, because the government of her country considered her a terrorist, the U.S. government was also officially required to treat her as a terrorist too. Due to the political quagmire of her situation, and because she also was an illegal alien under U.S. law, she had been in the El Paso detention center waiting for a resolution of her status for over *two years*!

At the time of writing this book, the United States is going through a huge controversy regarding immigration. A lot of people have gotten very emotional about this issue, but I don't think many have witnessed first hand the way people who are attempting to find a better way of life have been treated by our government the way Yo and I have. I have already expressed my views on the subject fairly extensively in this book, so I won't try to rehash it at this point. I do hope, however, that whoever reads this book is able to see a different perspective on the subject and understand that very few things in life are as cut and dried as we sometimes pretend they are.

The immigration problem is definitely controver-sial, but I for one have to believe there is a solution if people are willing to work together and try to find a common ground based on common sense. Whether or not we do is something that we may find out very soon, since it is one of the biggest issues, if not the *biggest* issue in the next presidential election. I would like to think that we, as a country, can try to find a solution that will not only maintain our national security, but also find a way to allow *all* people to seek a better way of life peacefully and to treat everyone with dignity and respect—even if they're *not* American citizens.

The day may come when some of us could also be desperate to find a new way of life. Most of us have not had to go through that experience. Think about it—when was the last time you were really **_desperate_**? What would **_you_** have done to provide for yourself or your family?

If it does ever happen to you—and I sincerely hope it doesn't—I would think you would want the powers that be to have a more compassionate and humane view towards your plight than they have to the people in that situation now.

Do you want it to change?

It's all up to you.